OHIO UNIVERSITY LIBRARY

Please return this book as soon as you have finished with it. In order to avoid a fine it must be returned by the latest date stamped below.

THE SONG OF DEEDS

THE SONG OF DEEDS

A STUDY OF *THE ANATHEMATA*
OF DAVID JONES

Neil Corcoran

CARDIFF
UNIVERSITY OF WALES PRESS
1982

© *University of Wales 1982*

British Library Cataloguing in Publication Data

Corcoran, Neil
    The song of deeds.
    1. Jones, David, *1895—1974*. Anathemata
    I. Title
    821.912   PR6019.053A/
    ISBN 0 7083 0806 6

This volume is published with the support
of the Welsh Arts Council.

*All rights reserved. No part of this book may be reproduced,
stored in a retrieval system, or transmitted, in any form or by any means,
electronic, mechanical, photocopying, recording or otherwise,
without clearance from the University of Wales Press.*

Printed by Bridgend Printing Company Limited, Bridgend, Mid Glamorgan.

For Gillian

Preface

The Anathemata, first published in 1952, has always been admired, particularly by other poets. Eliot thought it the 'remarkable' work of a writer 'of major importance';[1] and Auden, who wrote two lengthy, celebratory reviews of it, acknowledged it as 'the greatest long poem written in English in this century' and referred to David Jones as 'one of those elder modern poets from whom I have learned most'.[2]

Nevertheless, it was possible for a critic to write of Jones in 1967 that his reputation was then in the same state as Hopkins's had been forty years previously, 'known but not assimilated'.[3] And, although the study of Jones's work developed and deepened during the seventies, this lack of real assimilation was confirmed as late as 1980 when his publishers entitled a selection of his work *Introducing David Jones*. Protracted introductions consort oddly with enthusiastic recommendations and they create particular problems for the critic of the work. A preliminary word, then, on my own response to these problems.

The Anathemata is a difficult poem in some of the ways in which we expect modernist poems to be difficult: it is densely allusive and formally elusive. Jones's strategy of self-annotation is, in part, a response to this difficulty; but, until 1977, the ordinary reader lacked any further exegetical account of the poem. In that year René Hague's excellent commentary was published',[4] and this relieves the present study of the necessity for detailed explanatory comment. What straightforward explication I do attempt is to be found almost entirely in my third chapter.

But *The Anathemata* is also difficult in ways that the reader of modern poetry can be forgiven for finding harder to come to terms with. The range of its preoccupations and interests includes areas which many of its readers will inevitably find recondite, esoteric and perhaps eccentric. It is, in particular, a poem that displays an interest in Celtic mythology and in Roman Catholic sacramental theology and liturgy. My intention in this study—a critical, not an exegetical intention—is, in part, to suggest the ways in which some things that initially seem eccentric in David Jones can relocate themselves much closer to the centre of our most familiar concerns and preoccupations. I hope to show how and where an entry into this difficult poetry is likely to be effected for the unprejudiced reader; and I want to suggest why such a reader should think this effort worthwhile. This study will be successful if it achieves further recognition for John Holloway's insistence that 'Without Jones, the design of modern poetry has a hole in it.'[5]

But I hope, too, that my remarks are not over-assertive or over-emphatic. It is obvious to me that there can be no substitute for a sustained continuity of critical debate. A work that remains 'unassimilated' for any length of time after its publication develops a patina of unapproachability which is not easily rubbed off. In what follows in this book, I hope that a sense of regret and anxiety about the lack of this sustaining critical context, and about the dangers of limitation and exclusivity inherent in the *coterie* interest which Jones's work *has* sometimes attracted, can be seen to inform my own efforts at understanding and situating.

'Good commentaries', said Eliot, 'can be very helpful; but to study even the best commentary on a work of literary art is likely to be a waste of time unless we have first read and been excited by the text commented upon, even without understanding it.'[6] That 'thrill of excitement' of which Eliot goes on to speak is one which many good readers of *The Anathemata* have clearly felt, and David Jones's work needs no apologies. But it is, equally clearly, one which some good readers of poetry have not felt. This present study cannot supply excitement where it does not exist: but it can chastisedly acknowledge that it may not; and it can also, I hope, account for it intelligently where it does.

I am grateful to various people for their help in various ways: to Basil Bunting, Douglas Cleverdon, the late René Hague, Nicolas Jacobs, John Montague, David O'Neill, Nancy Sandars and Michael Walsh. Seamus Heaney has very kindly given permission to quote from a private letter to me. I am indebted also to the University of Sheffield for a grant from its Research Fund. Above all, I want to thank Peter Levi for his advice and encouragement when he read most of this book in an earlier form.

But my greatest debt is acknowledged by my dedication: without my wife, this book would not have been written.

Sheffield, January 1981   Neil Corcoran

Notes

1. 'A Note on "In Parenthesis" and "The Anathemata" ', *Dock Leaves*, VI no.4, Spring 1955, 21-23.
2. *A Certain World* (London, 1971), pp. 372, 373.
3. William T. Noon S. J., *Poetry and Prayer* (New Brunswick, 1967), p. 226.
4. *A Commentary on The Anathemata of David Jones* (Wellingborough, 1977).
5. *The Colours of Clarity* (London, 1964), p. 114.
6. 'A Note of Introduction', *In Parenthesis* (1963 edn.), p. viii. This introduction does not appear in the original edition of the poem.

Acknowledgements

The author and publishers gratefully acknowledge the permission granted by the following to reproduce the extracts noted:

Extracts from *The Anathemata* by David Jones are reprinted by permission of Faber and Faber Limited, London; copyright, 1952, by David Jones. The extract from Canto LXXVI in *The Cantos of Ezra Pound* by Ezra Pound is reprinted by permission of Faber and Faber Limited, London and New Directions Publishing Corporation, New York; copyright, 1948, by Ezra Pound. The extracts from 'Little Gidding' in *Four Quartets* by T. S. Eliot are reprinted by permission of Faber and Faber Limited, London, and Harcourt Brace Jovanovich, Inc., New York; copyright, 1943, by T. S. Eliot, renewed, 1971, by Esme Valerie Eliot. The extract from *Finnegans Wake* by James Joyce is reprinted by permission of The Society of Authors, London, as the literary representative of the Estate of James Joyce. The extract from 'Compline' in *Collected Poems* by W. H. Auden, edited by Edward Mendelson, is reprinted by permission of Faber and Faber Limited, London, and Random House Inc., New York; copyright, 1976, by Edward Mendelson, William Meredith and Monroe K. Spears, executors of the Estate of W. H. Auden. The extract from *The Use of Poetry and the Use of Criticism* by T. S. Eliot is reprinted by permission of Faber and Faber Limited, London and Harvard University Press, Cambridge, Massachusetts; copyright, 1933, by T. S. Eliot. 'Bone Dreams, III' by Seamus Heaney is reprinted by permission of Faber and Faber Limited, London (from *North*) and Farrar, Straus and Giroux, Inc., New York (from *Poems 1965-1975*); copyright, 1975, by Seamus Heaney.

Contents

		Page
Abbreviations		xii
I	A Gloss on the Book: The Intellectual Context of the Poem	1
II	Alone in Pellam's Land: The Genesis of the Poem	25
III	Efficacious Signs: The 'Content' of the Poem	42
IV	Making This Thing Other: The 'Form' of the Poem	75
V	Returning to the Origin: The Achievement of the Poem	94
Bibliography		115
Index		119

Abbreviations

(For editions used see Notes)

Ana *The Anathemata*
EA *Epoch and Artist*
Gaul *The Dying Gaul and Other Writings*
IP *In Parenthesis*
SL *The Sleeping Lord and Other Fragments*

CHAPTER I

A Gloss on the Book:
The Intellectual Context of the Poem

> First, a routine word
>   a gloss on the book
> and no more . . .
>
>   David Jones, *The Tribune's Visitation*

Reviewing Gilchrist's *Life of Blake* in 1866, James Thompson observed of the Prophetic Books that 'Every man living in seclusion and developing an intense interior life, gradually comes to give a quite peculiar significance to certain words and phrases and emblems.'[1] In this, even if in nothing else, like Blake, David Jones relies on such words and phrases and emblems, 'ships in which he has sailed over uncharted seas to unmapped shores.'[2] In an *oeuvre* quite exceptional for its unity and coherence, David Jones's poetry feeds symbiotically off his ideas, and *The Anathemata* depends, for real understanding, on an adequate sense of the background of theoretical speculation, of aesthetic and social discussion—often couched in an apparently private language of 'peculiar significance'—out of which it has grown. The elaborate preface to the poem, and the panoply of its annotation, testify to the fact that *The Anathemata* in no sense operates as a closed system; it constantly invites, prompts and encourages further speculation, outside its own immediate sphere of reference. It is a poem urgently, self-consciously and deliberately responsive to a large defining context of ideas, a context in which its own creation is the nodal point of interest. John Berryman, at the time himself at work on the long poem that was to become *The Dream Songs,* noted in a review of *The Anathemata* on its first American publication, that the preface contains 'a penetrating account of the Himalayan difficulties confronting an ambitious modern poet attempting a long poem';[3] and the air the poem sometimes has of being joyfully bewildered by its own existence is a fundamental part of its effect and meaning. The 'Himalayan difficulties' of the modern long poem, to which *The Anathemata* responds, as John Holloway has argued, on 'a scale commensurate with what is at issue',[4] are matters of sharp focus and, one might say, of acute discomfort, in the poem itself. *The Anathemata* is, crucially, a poem about its own possibility.

David Jones's perception of the complex issues involved in the making of a long poem is intimately connected with his sense of the crisis in modern European civilisation in which ' "man-the-artist" and "man-the-priest" become increasingly, in a sense, Ishmaels, or men of a kind of diaspora.'[5] His prose writings, collected in *Epoch and Artist* (1959) and in the posthumous *The Dying Gaul and Other Writings* (1978) are, all of them, in one way or another, attempts to describe the nature of this crisis, to understand what it means for the artist (not just the literary artist), and to formulate a response. His ultimate response is *The Anathemata* itself and, indeed, there is a radical continuity between the procedures of the prose and those of the poetry. The prose, at moments of heightened intensity, begins to take on the characteristic rhythms and cadences, and the energetic concretion, the 'haecceity',[6] of the poetry. The process is visible at its most obvious in this passage from the essay on the Roman roads, 'The Viae', where Jones, re-imagining the circumstances of the making of the roads, invites us to conjure up in our minds an image of the Roman soldiers at work who inevitably recall to him the trench-workers of the First World War:

> So our fatigue party is using some such implements to ram home in succession sub-foundation, foundation, pitching and surfacing. And each down-jolted double thumb vibrates the hidden syncline to where the chalk again outcrops far side the marly valley.
> The blackthorn is out and the thrush sings but though she is in April there are no English there. Beneath the starry, white-budded, black bough of the windy tree he sits on a pile of white rubble eyeing a work in progress. His rainproof cloak is of fine-wove British goat-hair fabric, in Silchester-dyed cockle-red; an export market product.[7]

This linguistic exuberance—mannered, perhaps, but usually well-mannered too, knowing its own limits, 'pitching and surfacing'—is the signature of David Jones's prose. It is also a measure of its frequent opacity. The reader is held up on it, usually admiringly but sometimes irritatedly, and it can seem far from the transparency and lucidity we might naturally expect from discursive prose.

This local verbal opacity is sometimes linked to what Jones himself, nervously aware of the possible objection, calls 'a certain catlike obliqueness of direction, and the leaving of this scent for that' and, elsewhere, somewhat reductively, 'these meanderings'.[8] The generous humility and tentativeness of the venture are insisted by the apologies; but the apologies, sometimes circling on themselves in slightly baffled comment on the whole procedure, serve, of course, only to slow things up even further. David Jones must be regarded, even in his prose of explication and argument, as an imaginative and intuitive writer. If the intuition is always disciplined by scholarship, the essays are, nevertheless, a process of discovery, not the presentation of a set of resolutions and conclusions. Reading a David Jones essay is an immersion, a surrender, and a gradual, almost imperceptible enrichment; it is very much, in fact, like reading a poem. In this alone, Jones reveals, stylistically, an indebtedness to Ruskin and Morris, neither of whom could be considered often capable of lucidly advancing a prose argument. Indeed, what Kenneth Clark has said about Ruskin, that 'in his mind, as in the eye of an impressionist painter, everything was more or less reflected in everything else; and when he tries too hard to keep his mind in a single track . . . some of its beautiful colour is lost',[9] could with as much justice be said about Jones. He is not secure in generalisation; he is weak in analytic thought; he tends to the repetitive and over-insistent; he is not a *systematic* thinker. The writings manifest everywhere both the quirky individuality and the cunning ingenuity of autodidactic effort and ambition. But the obvious difficulty with which his thought expresses itself may be taken as an index of its depth. In this chapter, I want to describe the colour of that thought, to trace its points of reference and its analogues, to set its context, and to examine the 'peculiar significance' which Jones attaches to his most important and recurring 'words and phrases and emblems', as a necessary preliminary stage in the study of the poem that is the formal embodiment of that thought in art.

In the 'Note of Introduction' which he wrote for the paperback edition of *In Parenthesis* in 1963, T. S. Eliot discovered in Jones's work 'some affinity with that of James Joyce . . . and with the later work of Ezra Pound, and with my own.' David Jones, he wrote, 'is a representative of the same literary generation as Joyce and Pound and myself.'[10] Jones is certainly intimately wedded to the modernist tradition Eliot is invoking here by the first premises of his argument with his own time. The sense of crisis conveyed in Jones's writings is basic and central to modernism. Donald Davie has shown, in *Ezra Pound, Poet as Sculptor*, how some concept of the Fall is an imaginative necessity for the generation Eliot characterises here: the sense of history informing their work is apocalyptic, and sees the present as a tragic falling off from some finer light (a process initiated, for Pound, somewhere between Cavalcanti and Petrarch, for Yeats about 1550, and for Eliot himself, with his 'dissociation of sensibility', between 1590 and 1650). As Frank Kermode has stressed in his influential study, *The Sense of an Ending*, eschatological anxiety, the mood of end-dominated crisis, is endemic to modernism. And David Jones has his own personal brand of it. It is a synthetic brand, drawing its deepest terrors, as the Yeats of *A Vision* tells us his 'instructors' drew theirs, from the shrill Germanic desperation of Spengler's *The Decline of the West* (Jones recognises in

Spengler 'a kind of satisfaction at the grimness of our destiny'[11]), but taking most of its form and vocabulary from a Roman Catholic extension and application of a complex of ideas discovered in William Morris and John Ruskin.

It has been suggested that Jones did not follow Spengler at any theoretical level, but was impressed and haunted by his 'disturbed visions'.[12] It is certainly true that Jones's whole enterprise is hostile to Spengler's conclusions about the irreversible hardening of a culture into a civilisation (although Jones does find the distinction itself 'useful' and 'valid'[13]), and to his commitment to a policy of 'technics instead of lyrics';[14] but certain of Spengler's theories and formulations are obviously vital to Jones. Spengler, he writes in 'The Myth of Arthur', 'had very special insight into the cyclic character of the periods of decline, and certainly the trend, so far as we can see, of the contemporary world, verifies a number of his conclusions.'[15] Spengler's presumption that we are living on 'the metaphysically-exhausted soil of the West'[16] is echoed, and taken for granted, throughout Jones's work, and receives its fullest expression in *The Anathemata* itself at the end of 'Angle-Land', where the Second World War is set 'toward the last phase/of our dear West.'[17] The sense of 'eschatological anxiety' that embodies itself in Spengler's concept of the 'epoch', in which events mark in the course of a culture 'a necessary and fateful turning-point',[18] is implicit in Jones's use of the term and is taken seriously enough as a definition of his own time to provide the title for Jones's first collection of essays, *Epoch and Artist*. And Spengler's image of a culture as a 'personality' going through its youth, middle age and gradual hardening of the arteries before its decay into a civilisation, is reflected in Jones's naming the European Middle Ages 'the young-time'[19] and his sense of the modern period as a 'cultural December'.[20] In lesser matters—the use of the Apollinian-Magian-Faustian distinction as cultural description[21] and the concept of the 'man of fact' as the true inheritor of a decadent civilisation[22]—Jones also follows Spengler.

It is easy to see why critics should be eager to protect Jones from too great an identification with the corrosively amoral pessimism of Spengler, but these do, indeed, seem to be significant debts at a theoretical and speculative level. Although in what follows I shall be describing the very different road Jones takes away from Spengler's brutally over-simplified conclusions, it is nevertheless useful to remind ourselves of something Northrop Frye expresses succinctly when he says that Spengler's 'paralleling of our historical situation with earlier periods, especially that of the Roman Empire, and his point that our technology could be part of a decline as easily as it could be part of an advance, are conceptions that we all accept now, as something which is inseparably part of our perspective.'[23] It is also, perhaps, useful to remember that a social critic in many ways antipodeanly different from Jones, F. R. Leavis, insisted in *For Continuity* that Spengler had indeed grasped the 'fundamental nature' of the problem of industrialism. 'One can,' Leavis said, 'without endorsing the Spenglerian idiom or philosophy, recognize its felicity . . . as an account of the present situation. The traditional ways of life have been destroyed by the machine, more and more does human life depart from the natural rhythms, the cultures have mingled, and the forms have dissolved into chaos, so that everywhere the serious literature of the West betrays a sense of paralysing consciousness, of a lack of direction, of momentum, of dynamic axioms.'[24] If for 'literature' here we substituted 'arts', the thought would be exactly David Jones's. So that the most intelligent way of suggesting the relationship with Spengler might be to claim that Jones found in him, at a time when he was formulating the thought behind his most important prose writings (a letter of 26 February 1942 finds Jones 'battling' with Spengler[25]), a verbal embodiment of a complex of ideas and attitudes that seemed to Jones, as to many of his generation, accurately to locate modern European civilisation in what Spengler, throughout *The Decline of the West*, refers to as the 'morphology of world-culture'. Modern Europe had reached, through its technological advance, a point of apparently terminal collapse in which a continuity and tradition of human value seemed impossible to sustain. Such a belief is as informingly axiomatic in Jones as it is in Spengler.

For Jones, however, as for Leavis, the assent to Spengler involves no pessimistic acceptance of such operative conditions but rather the pushing of all his intellectual and imaginative energies towards the creation, out of his own life and art, of a radical challenge to those conditions. It is in this challenge that the moral passion and strength, the exemplary refusal, of David Jones's achievement is to be found. Taking Spengler's dystopian analysis for granted, Jones faces, as Seamus Heaney has claimed, 'singlehanded, the task of creating a British counter-culture.'[26] The weft of this challenge is a personal—and, perhaps, idiosyncratic—fusion of Roman Catholic sacramental theology and aesthetic theory; its warp is an alternately joyful and wearily defeated sense of the ancient cultural unity that was the 'Island of Britain' which focusses on what Jones calls in 'The Welsh Dragon', 'Celticity',[27] the reality and 'idea' of Wales. The material spun from these fibres might seem an extraordinarily esoteric and anachronistic one to cover the needs of a twentieth-century writer; and it is certainly true that David Jones's writings can, at times, seem fussily pedantic and programmatic. But it is worth noting that a contemporary critical theorist as influential as Harold Rosenberg, author of *The Tradition of the*

New, wrote what Jones himself considered the only really understanding review of *Epoch and Artist*, and described the book, in 1964, as 'some of the most acutely relevant writing on contemporary form and value to have appeared in years.'[28] ('Relevant' for Rosenberg meant relevant even to the New York abstract expressionists and action painters of the fifties and early sixties.) For all the apparently esoteric eclecticism of his scholarship and sources, David Jones managed to formulate an account of the artist in his relation to contemporary civilisation that seems inescapably compelling and, given the Spenglerian premises of his argument, deeply positive and affirming. Despite their root-obsession with 'ends', David Jones's writings employ elegy as only one of their many modes. In what follows, I am examining the fusions which have made possible such difficult affirmations.

The precise focus of Jones's argument with the present is that modern technology has robbed us of a tradition of human value realised, or made incarnate, in art; we live in an age in which the whole tendency and thrust is 'for creativeness to become dehumanized, for contrivance to usurp imagination, for the will toward shape to become almost indistinguishable from a mere will toward power.'[29] In this concentration on what the processes inaugurated by the Industrial Revolution have meant for the practice of an art, David Jones's thought, and its expression, deliberately remove themselves from Spengler and reveal instead an immersion in the less rhetorically assertive discourse of Ruskin and Morris. In the preface to *The Anathemata*, Jones's term for his sense of cultural and historical dislocation, a term that carries in his work the sort of force that the phrase, 'dissociation of sensibility', carries in Eliot's, is 'The Break'; and Colin Wilcockson has—to my mind, conclusively—demonstrated that this is a reminiscence, probably unconscious, of Morris's image in his essay, 'The Beauty of Life', of 'a break in the continuity of the golden chain' which binds us to our past.[30] For Jones, the origins of this 'Break' are to be found in nineteenth-century industrialism, in which the ancient unity of the beautiful and the useful was severed, and the 'gratuitous' quality which ought to inhere in all human making was destroyed by the capacity of a machine culture to produce only utilitarian goods, what Jones refers to as 'the utile'. This distinction between the 'gratuitous' and the 'utile' is influenced by Ruskin's 'The Relation of Art to Use' and by Morris's *Lectures on Art and Industry*.[31] But, in David Jones, this tradition is refracted through a response to, and a modification of, the ideas of Eric Gill, whose attempt at a Ruskinian community of craftsmen at Ditchling in Sussex and, later, at Capel-y-ffin in mid-Wales Jones was associated with in the 1920s.[32]

Apart from the importance of his contact with Gill in the formation of David Jones's ideas, this period spent in a community of practising artists, or 'craftsmen', was vital to his lasting sense of the importance of the 'contactual' in all thinking about art. His aesthetic discussion is, as it were, justified and sanctioned by his own practice as a 'maker'. For David Jones, it is in this 'contact' with his material that the artist releases his true humanity. 'Ars is adamant about one thing,' he insists: 'she compels you to do an infantryman's job. She insists on the tactile. The artist in man is the infantryman in man, so that . . . all men are aboriginally *of* this infantry, though not all serve *with* this infantry.'[33] This characteristic military metaphor is Jones's version of an idea inherited directly from Gill, that 'the artist is not a special kind of man, but every man is a special kind of artist.'[34] Hence, for David Jones, the technology which prevents man from realising his capacity as an artist prevents him also, *ipso facto*, from realising himself as a man. To be rendered incapable of performing 'the sole intransitive activity of man',[35] and of performing it with a gratuitous joy, is to be made, quite literally, inhuman. 'By a sort of paradox,' Jones says, 'man can act gratuitously only because he is dedicated to the gods. When he falls from dedication he again acts like an animal—the utile is all he knows and his works take on something of the nature of the works of the termites.'[36] This is the measure of the problem to which David Jones addresses himself: he must find, in an age apparently radically hostile to the whole enterprise, some way of re-establishing a sense of human value and of embodying that value in his own art. For it is axiomatic that 'the more man behaves as artist and the more the artist in man determines the whole shape of his behaviour, so much the more is he Man.'[37]

It is profoundly significant, then, that Jones's primary sense of the importance of the Catholic tradition is its celebration of the contactual. It 'commits its adherents,' he writes, 'in a most inescapable manner, to the body and the embodied; hence to history, to locality, to epoch and site, to sense-perception, to the contactual, the known, the felt, the seen, the handled, the cared for, the tended, the conserved; to the qualitative and to the intimate.'[38] Catholicism, for Jones, is a religion 'explicitly dependent upon small, intimate, enclosed, known and dear creaturely signs' and man, in his true and essential nature, is 'the only extra-utilist, or sacramentalist.'[39] It is in the construction of a sacramental theory of artistic representation, or 're-presentation', that Jones's real originality as a theorist is to be found, and it is a theory that provides the context for, and often the actual vocabulary of, his own poetry. If there is truth in the idea that Jones's Catholicism is a very heterodox mixture, more or less made by him to his own measure, it is also true nevertheless that it inspires him, in a wholly traditional way, as it inspired Joyce and Hopkins before him, into a vivid sense of the world as the theatre of encoded, but decipherable, significance. The world in Hopkins, 'charged with the grandeur of God', is a drama of inscape; in Joyce's *Finnegans Wake*, it 'is, was and will be writing its own wrunes for ever, man'; and in David Jones it is an organisation of 'signs' which it is the artist's duty, and delight, to search out and celebrate.

At the opening of *The Anathemata*, the representative priest/artist figure is discovered lifting up 'an efficacious sign' and guarding 'the *signa*'. This is, for David Jones, the essential act of celebration and preservation lying at the root of his understanding of the nature of art. The artist is one whose business is the recovery and transmission of those moments and acts and qualities of being which, in his own culture and inheritance, most transparently evoke certain sorts of 'otherness'. The central concept of the 'sign' in David Jones involves all that we usually understand by 'symbol', but points beyond this, too, to a specifically Christian sense of the sacramental nature of human reality, of the transforming and informing presence in human affairs and in human history of the fact of 'incarnation'. (It should perhaps be said that Jones's use of the term 'sign' bears no immediate relation to the most famous contemporary use of the word, in structuralist theory.) Present to all of Jones's thinking on the subject is the work of Jacques Maritain, especially his *Art et Scolastique* which Jones's friend John O'Connor translated in 1923 and which the Gill community treated with reverential respect.[40] Maritain's book is, essentially, a drawing out of the aesthetic theory which he finds implicit in Aquinas and scholasticism. It is an endeavour full of subtle philosophical discrimination coloured every so often by a grand high style, not altogether unlike the kind of theorising which Joyce puts into the mouth (and mind) of Stephen Dedalus in *A Portrait of the Artist as a Young Man*.

Maritain's theory certainly provides a context for Jones's thought. His refusal, in *Art et Scolastique*, to divorce 'artist' and 'artisan'; his belief that 'art is a *habitus* of the practical understanding'; his analysis of the relative rights of 'Ars' and 'Prudentia'; his refusal to consider art as mimesis, but to assert, rather, that it consists 'in making, composing, or constructing, and that according to the laws of the object itself to be set up in being (whether it be ship, house, carpet, coloured cloth or carven block)': all are of central importance in Jones's own work.[41] But it would be completely wrong to think of David Jones's essays as, in any sense, merely applied Maritain. When Maritain is present in them, it is, as Frank Kermode has pointed out in an essay on Jones, 'Maritain thought and felt and disagreed with'.[42] It is rather that Jones who, like Joyce, had already come to an appreciation of the coherence and practical descriptive usefulness of the scholastic synthesis, found in Maritain an indication of the ways in which this coherence could speak, clarifyingly and liberatingly, to his own position as a modern artist and, indeed, to the nature of the arts in the twentieth century. The scholastic philosophy developed and adopted for its theology by Catholicism, and emphasised by the neo-Thomist revival in the English Catholic circles in which Jones moved from the 1920s, had the great value of being 'consonant with man as a sign-making animal.'[43] Maritain seemed to show how it was possible to heal the wound in human consciousness made by the Industrial Revolution; his work acts as a bridge that joins the world of the scholastics to the world of the moderns at the centre of his argument, Cézanne, Rouault, Baudelaire and Satie. And this function of unification is the essential spur to Jones's own development of theory.

The main inspiration behind Jones's evolution of the concept of the 'sign' was not Maritain, however, but the French theologian Maurice de la Taille, whose *Mysterium Fidei* Jones was aware of in some form from 1926, and which he actually read in 1934.[44] De la Taille defines a sacrament as 'a symbol that effects by itself in the mind what it signifies',[45] his version of the Church's traditional definition of a sacrament as *signum efficax*—David Jones's 'efficacious sign'—which indicates, in strict theological terms, that a sacrament infuses divine grace in its recipient. For David Jones, by an analogy which is more than just an analogy, the 'signs' he gathers together are intended, similarly, to effect by themselves in the mind what they signify. It is the idea of evoking, almost tangibly, a symbolised reality, that Jones wishes the word 'sign' to suggest.

The centre of de la Taille's speculations is to be found in his discussion of the institution of the eucharist. Here, he understands Christ to have done, literally, in *fact*, on the hill of Calvary, what he had already done symbolically, or in 'sign', in the Upper Room of Maundy Thursday, and what he orders the Church to do, in memory of him, throughout history. Christ is, then, understood by David Jones as doing in the institution of the eucharist what it is the essence of all art to do—symbolising, transforming, and ensuring future preservation. It is thus that Christ, in the phrase from de la Taille which Jones uses as epigraph to *Epoch and Artist*, 'placed Himself in the order of signs.'[46] This theological 'order of signs' is taken over by Jones as the natural territory and preserve of the artist; he extends and develops into an aesthetic theory what is, in de la Taille, a theological definition. As Jones says in one of his extended notes to the late poem, *The Fatigue*, de la Taille 'in the early 1920's open [ed] windows and made sense of relationships altogether outside the immediate context of his strictly theological thesis.'[47]

It is in de la Taille's understanding of the Roman mass and its sacramental, or sign-making, character that David Jones's theories are centred. The mass is, for Jones, itself an 'art work' which involves 'an intention to re-present, recall or show-forth something under certain signs and by manual acts.'[48] And this is also the intention of the artist engaged on a work: in Jones's theory, art becomes a showing forth, under other forms, of certain realities. The things man makes are 'signs of something other'; man is 'unavoidably a sacramentalist and . . . his works are sacramental in character.'[49] It is important to point out that, while this view of the processes of artistic creation has its foundations in a Catholic view of the nature of reality and while it is, at places in Jones's work, explicitly Christian in its orientation, it is nevertheless an attempt to understand and to describe, without specific theological prejudice, the true nature of all artefacture. For David Jones, art is, in its essential nature, a 'religious' activity; and his sense of the world as a complex organisation of significance constitutes a radical argument with what he sees as the reductive and destructive tendencies of nominalist and positivist theory. The vocabulary he borrows for his own formulations is as much a stance for combat as the myth of history he espouses is a battle with the nineteenth century myth of progress.

In this world charged with significance, it is the artist's responsibility to search out, and to re-present, 'valid signs', and the very title of the poem to which this study is devoted is an emphatic affirmation of such responsibility. In Jones's essays, the word 'anathemata' is used almost interchangeably, and synonymously, with the words 'signs' and 'signa'. The poem, *The Anathemata*, is, then, a gathering together of certain 'signs' radiant with 'otherness' which demand from David Jones evocation for, and re-presentation to, his readers; and it is natural that it is the poem's preface that gives us the fullest and most helpful definition of his essential meaning. The 'anathemata' are, he tells us there,

> the blessed things that have taken on what is cursed and the profane things that somehow are redeemed: the delights and also the 'ornaments', both in the primary sense of gear and paraphernalia and in the sense of what simply adorns; the donated and votive things, the things dedicated after whatever fashion, the things in some sense made separate, being 'laid up from other things'; things, or some aspect of them, that partake of the extra-utile and of the gratuitous; things that are the signs of something other, together with those signs that not only have the nature of a sign, but are themselves, under some mode, what they signify. Things set up, lifted up, or in whatever manner made over to the gods. (*Ana*, 28-29)

This essential act of evoking and re-presenting is particularly incumbent upon the poet whose medium, language, is inevitably the most open and socially contingent of all artistic media. The poet must act, Jones believes, as a 'rememberer': in art there is always, he says in the major essay, 'Art and

Sacrament', 'a recalling, a re-presenting again, anaphora, anamnesis.'[50] The word 'anamnesis' is used throughout Jones's work, and in the text of *The Anathemata* itself, in a way exactly analogous to his use of the word 'sign'. Jones relies for his understanding of the term on another theological work profoundly influential on his thought, Gregory Dix's huge study of the Church's worship, *The Shape of the Liturgy*, although he would also have met the word in Spengler, who cites Plato's use of it.[51] In Dix, it is discussed as the word used in the Greek scriptures for Christ's eucharistic command, 'Do this in memory of me', 'Do this for my anamnesis'. The definition of the word given by Dix, 'a "recalling" or "re-presenting" before God of an event in the past, so that it becomes *here and now operative by its effects*',[52] is closely allied to Jones's own definition of 'sign', and 'anamnesis' is a term that could, obviously, have been invented for his purpose. When he uses it, he is insisting that the signs or anathemata which he makes over to the gods in his own work are intended to be evoked and re-presented with such an intensity of reverential remembrance that they become a living, incarnate reality and an embodiment of a dense recession of human values, attachments and significations. Whether David Jones's signs are drawn from pre-history and the processes of the world's geology, or from the course of human history, or from particular tracts of known territory, or from the arts, religions and myths of mankind, they are all intended to confront us with the essential realities of these re-imagined worlds and data. The loving, patient dedication with which they are re-called in *The Anathemata* is intended to re-establish a sense of their inherent dignity and beauty and formal splendour. The meanings they 'incant' (another Jonesian term) are uncovered and sung in the work.

The process of anamnesis is one to which all poets are, in David Jones's view, inescapably committed by the nature of their art, however personal or directly autobiographical their work might be. Once an experience has occurred, Jones observes in 'Past and Present', 'a "deed" has entered history ... and is therefore valid as matter for our poetry. For poetry is the song of deeds.'[53] This Englishing of the French *chanson de geste* is obviously intelligible, and memorably so, as a definition of poetry; but it is also a gesture towards the fact that the sort of poetry Jones wishes to write himself is dependent on the evocation and 'anamnesis' of far more than his own individual experience. 'It seems to me,' he says, 'that a deed that entered history a millenium, or fifty milleniums, ago and which has been assimilated into the mythos of whole groups of men, perhaps of the whole group called mankind, is, *other things being equal*, of even more validity for our poetry.' It is the duty of the poet, as 'rememberer', to 'keep open the lines of communication' with the past. And, believing that 'the artist is not responsible *for* the future but he is, in a certain sense, responsible *to* the future', Jones thinks that the way in which these lines might best be kept open by the poet is 'by handing on such fragmented bits of our own inheritance as we have ourselves received.'[54] What Jones means by an 'inheritance' here—and the word is also importantly placed at the opening of the preface to *The Anathemata*, where the poet's function is described as the 'showing forth of an inheritance'—is very close to what Eliot means by the word 'tradition' in that most seminal of all his essays, 'Tradition and the Individual Talent'. Jones's view of the poet as 'rememberer' is a response to the same sense of historical crisis that informs, and anguishes, Eliot's work, a crisis defined by Hugh Kenner, in a study of modernism, when he observes that 'Civilization is memory, and after 1918 effective memory was almost lost.'[55]

It is this desire to preserve some trace of 'effective memory' that David Jones shares in common with Eliot, and it touches the heart of his beliefs about the nature of art and about the relationship between the artist and his society. For the concept is drawn from the traditional function of the poet in an organic, pre-industrial community, where he was 'explicitly and by profession the custodian, rememberer, embodier and voice of the mythus, etc., of some contained group of families, or of a tribe, nation, people, cult.' (*Ana*, 21) Roger Kojecky has pointed to the importance in Eliot's poetic theory of a sense of the origins and development of literature in 'a kind of state of nature in which the poet is the point of maximum consciousness of a close-knit society.'[56] And in Eliot's *The Use of Poetry and the Use of Criticism*, the poet in such a community is seen as a prophetic or priestly figure, and poetry is described as 'the expression of the mind of a whole people.'[57] This residual strain in both Eliot and Jones towards a sense of the poet as the unselfconscious conveyor of a tradition, or an inheritance, integrated in his community and respected as essential to the health of his culture, is a spectre evoked nostalgically at the feasts of the critical writings of both men. But Eliot's famous chemical image ('I therefore invite you to consider . . .') of the poet's mind as 'a receptacle for seizing and storing up numberless feelings, phrases, images, which remain there until all the particles which can unite to form a new compound are present together',[58] makes the function of 'remembering' much less specific and less conscious, and much less a matter of social responsibility, than Jones's view of the poet as 'something of a vicar whose job is legatine—a kind of Servus Servorum to deliver what has been delivered to him, who can neither add to nor take from the deposits.' (*Ana*, 35)

Jones's insistence on the poet's necessary impersonality in this function is also more rigorous than Eliot's. The anti-Romantic bias is clearly apparent in Jones when he thinks of the poet as a 'workman' piecing together a 'shape' from various bits of material. 'When the workman is dead,' he writes, 'the only thing that will matter is the work, objectively considered. Moreover, the workman must be dead to himself while engaged upon the work, otherwise we have that sort of "self-expression" which is as undesirable in the painter or in the writer as in the carpenter, the cantor, the half-back, or the cook.' (*Ana*, 12) It is a theoretical necessity that Jones, attempting to restore, in his own work, something of the medieval synthesis that made no distinction between 'art' and 'craft', and concerned with the purity of his own poetic motive as the agent of 'effective memory', should think in these terms; and his views, though certainly influenced in some of their details by Eliot's, should not be thought directly indebted to the older poet. They are, rather, Jones's personal elaboration of a general context of ideas—Catholic, modernist, anthropological—prevalent in the circles with which both he and Eliot had contact.[59] In Jones, as in Eliot, the practice is sometimes rather different from the theory; but, in Jones, the theory does provide a necessary intellectual rationale for the whole undertaking.

The nostalgia for an organic community in which the poet could act unselfconsciously as a rememberer is part of the compulsion behind Jones's handing on of his Welsh 'inheritance'. The respective 'falls' which I characterised earlier as endemic to modernist writing are all falls from an imagined Edenic state in which the poet, or artist, was integrated in his community in something of this manner: hence Yeats's Byzantium, Pound's Provence and Cathay, and what Frank Kermode has called Eliot's 'nostalgia for closed, immobile, hierarchical societies.'[60] 'Wales' in David Jones's work, or at least the territory of the primitive and Romanized Celtic communities, has something of the force that 'Byzantium' has in Yeats, 'Provence' in Pound; but the full implications of the Celtic in David Jones extend much further than this, and I want, now, to examine them in some detail.

In an essay on Eric Gill, David Jones writes that Gill 'sought to work as though a culture of some sort existed or, at all events, he worked as though one should, and could *make* a culture exist.'[61] Elsewhere, he observes that 'a culture is nothing but a sign, and the *anathemata* of a culture, "the things set up", can be set up only to the gods.'[62] The collection of signs that David Jones retrieves, and wishes to make 'here and now operative', might be regarded as his attempt to act as though one could '*make* a culture exist' in a megalopolitan, industrial civilisation. And the signs which Jones, as a Londoner and a Welshman, wishes to recover are intimately connected with what he calls, throughout his work, the 'deposits' of Britain, a rich, complex, corporate *mythus*. These deposits are necessary to Jones's poetry partly because it is the combination of Anglo-Saxon and Celt in his own blood that makes him what he is, but mainly because they incant, for Jones, an admirably integrated, unified, organic culture. They are, one might say, important to Jones in some of the same ways in which George Sturt's *The Wheelwright's Shop* was important in Leavis's early work: they provide a myth of unity and organicism in the light of which modern civilisation can be regarded as tragic deterioration. In Jones's desire to retrieve the signs of a rich, but lost, cultural inheritance, the things of Wales are central and basic.

Wales, of course, can never be merely idea and myth to David Jones—plastic and malleable and infinitely extensive—in the way that Byzantium, for instance, can remain idea and myth for Yeats, and Jones does not forget that the place of Wales in the 'Great Britain' of the twentieth century needs to be discussed in its actual political reality. But contemporary Wales, which Jones regards as plundered of its true culture by colonial and imperialist domination, is most often only the matter for elegy and lament, as it is throughout the 'Celtic' poems in *The Sleeping Lord and Other Fragments*, in the great inscription of 1959, *Cara Wallia Derelicta*, and, indeed, in *The Anathemata* itself where, in 'Rite and Fore-Time', the processes of geological formation are said to occur

> Before the slow estuarine alchemies had coal-blacked the green dryad-ways over the fire-clayed seat-earth along all the utile seams from Taff to Tâf.
> (*Ana*, 72)

There is, it would seem, little Jones can do with the South Wales coalfield other than to lament its robbery of the land's configurated beauty. And when he does write, in a rather bizarre piece, in support of a Plaid Cymru candidate in the 1974 election, he disclaims all direct political knowledge: 'I know nothing,' he says, 'of political affairs, of what policy should or should not be followed, but the only "message" I have is that the Welsh language is what matters.'[63]

And the language 'matters' for Jones because it incants a culture that 'belongs to the *mores* of all Britain, and affords a direct, living, unbroken series of links with Antiquity and so with the formative period and the foundational things of this land.'[64] The political reality of contemporary Wales matters to Jones in that its struggle to preserve a tradition is an immediate and pressing example of the fight to maintain continuity in a world always, and increasingly, hostile to the local and particular; but the 'idea' of Wales matters more to Jones in that it supplies him with a 'sign' of a lost integration and wholeness. *The Anathemata* is dedicated to recovering and celebrating this lost unity; and it is in this sense a 'political' poem. For David

Jones, 'Poetry is to be diagnosed as "dangerous" because it evokes and recalls, is a kind of *amamnesis* of . . . something loved. In that sense it is inevitably "propaganda", in that any real formal expression "propagands" the reality which caused those forms and their content to be.' (*Ana*, 21) 'The more real the thing,' he says, 'the more it will confound their politics.' (*Ana*, 22)

The poet, then, fulfils his political and social responsibility by handing on the *mythus* of his tribe, and by attempting to revalidate its lost signs. In his act of remembering, he is building what Jones characterises as a 'Boethian' bridge into the past of his own race.[65] A proper awareness of the past—'a perception', as Eliot has it, 'not only of the pastness of the past, but of its presence'[66]—is dependent, for Jones, on the sense of cultural identity truly possible only for those in direct, organic relationship with a particular territory. This strain in David Jones's thinking, which can seem programmatic and even fictional, based on no available cultural reality, should be seen against the background of the kinds of argument for social cohesion—in Eliot's *Notes towards the Definition of Culture* (1948), in Simone Weil's *L'Enracinement* (1949; translated in 1952 as *The Need for Roots*), in Christopher Dawson's *Religion and Culture* (1948)—which seem an inevitable product of the European mid-century and of minds conscious of the enormous human and cultural disruption of two world wars. Eliot's social theories may well seem a fiction when one considers how exceptionally cosmopolitan his life was, and how self-consciously international his poetry; and David Jones himself spent very little of his life actually living on the territory he celebrates so often. But Eliot is more tentative in his prescriptions than his critics sometimes make him seem, and Jones would certainly be in agreement with him when he rejects any 'artificially sustained antiquarianism' and decides that 'what is wanted is not to restore a vanished, or to revive a vanishing culture under modern conditions which make it impossible, but to grow a contemporary culture from the old roots.'[67] 'Uprooting', Simone Weil observes, 'breeds idolatry'; and David Jones's whole enterprise is dedicated to establishing what Weil calls 'the most important and least recognised need of the human soul'[68]—the need to be rooted.

It is, then, the urgency of his desire to uncover the roots of his Anglo-Celtic heritage that involves Jones intimately in the 'deposits' of early Welsh history and myth. These deposits are centred on the Welsh Arthurian cycle which Jones takes primarily from Geoffrey of Monmouth's *Historia Regum Britanniae* and from the collection which has come to be known as *The Mabinogion* (Jones was familiar with the versions of Lady Charlotte Guest [1877] and of Gwyn Jones and Thomas Jones [1949]), though he is also, of course, as *In Parenthesis* makes clear, intimate with the later stages of the cycle, particularly in the recension of Malory. The primary value of this material for Jones is stressed in a letter to Vernon Watkins where he says that it provides 'a connecting link between the tradition of Wales and that of England';[69] and, he says in 'The Arthurian Legend', it acts, beyond this unific function, as our great corporate European myth, 'an *Iliad-Aeneid* of the Celtic-Germano-Latin Christian medieval West.'[70] It connects us, that is, with our remotest origins as a tribe, and a crucial part of the appeal for Jones of the Welsh deposits is their sheer antiquity: ' "Whan that Aprille" was in England,' he tells us with the wry pride of one whose birth makes him a direct inheritor of both traditions, 'it was already past midsummer in Wales.'[71]

Because what Jones calls the Welsh 'thing' is embodied above all in its ancient language, he feels compelled to use that language in his own work. Discussing the matter in his letters, and in his doctoral address to the University of Wales, Jones reveals a deep sadness about his inability to speak the language. He knows intimately, he says, the 'pain of loss'[72] consequent upon this human and cultural diminishment and decides that his poetry must, in however attenuated a form, attempt to convey 'what, at its subtlest and best and most incantational, is locked up in the ancient tongue of Britain.'[73] This combination of Welsh language and Welsh deposits—the most ancient and venerable part of the mixed racial identity which is David Jones's by birth—is the point of greatest 'discomfort' in *The Anathemata*. The poem's form—I describe it later as a 'poem-with-notes'—is compelled largely by the necessity of educating readers in matters of pronunciation and otherwise almost inaccessible historical, legendary and mythical source material. If it is true, as we are told in the preface to the poem, that the artist must 'work within the limits of his love', it is surely also true that, if the reader is to respond properly, then for him, as for the poet, 'There must be no mugging-up, no "ought to know" or "try to feel".' (*Ana*, 24) And yet the proliferating annotation of *The Anathemata* is ample testimony to the fact that the ordinary reader of the poem is inevitably going to have to 'try to feel', and that David Jones realises this by showing himself willing, in his notes, to give as much opportunity for 'mugging-up' as he can.

But the importance of 'Wales' in Jones's work is even more problematical than this if one believes, along with René Hague, that there is, indeed, a certain amount of 'mugging-up' in David Jones's own knowledge of, and feeling for, these deposits. In his commentary on the poem, Hague observes that Jones's love of the Brythonic and Romanised Brythonic culture is 'artificially stimulated because, being cut off from Wales, D. had no roots reaching down into Welsh ways of thinking and speaking through which he could draw natural nourishment for his love.' Against this, he contrasts 'the poet's involvement—unconscious, natural and uncontrived—in the far richer tradition that came to England from Greece, Rome, the Saxon and Norman invasions and France.' We have to conclude, says Hague, 'that, for all his love of Wales, he is eminently an English poet. *The Battle of Maldon*, *The Dream of the Rood*, medieval English lyrics, *Piers Plowman*, Chaucer, folk-song, Malory, Shakespeare, Milton, Blake, Smart, Coleridge, Browning, Hopkins—these, and the classical world behind them, are the homeland of his tradition.'[74] This is, I think, very well said, and certainly redresses the sectarian, and sometimes rather embattled, enthusiasm with which Jones's work has been received in some circles. But perhaps it is a little *too* well said: David Jones himself would almost certainly never have accepted that the central English tradition was 'far richer' than the Celtic; and the reader of much of *The Anathemata*, certainly of Part VII, 'Mabinog's Liturgy', will not get far with only a classical/English area of reference. Nevertheless, most impartial readers do undoubtedly feel, as Hague does, the lack of a certain inwardness with his Welsh material in David Jones himself. I wish to conclude these observations on 'Wales' in David Jones with an attempt to explain how I think this lack is not a mere absence, a negative point of embarrassment for the critic of the poem, but an indication at the most profound level—that is, at the level of material and language—of the poem's most central meaning.

Something of what I wish to convey is suggested by David Jones himself when, in the autobiographical piece, 'In illo tempore', he describes his initial reaction to the Pergamon sculpture of the Dying Gaul:

> I naturally liked him, for he epitomized for me so much of Celtdom, or what little I knew of it in 1909-10. At least I sensed a continuity of struggle and a continuity of loss. I could not recall hearing of works celebrative of victory, but only of relentless resistance culminating in defeat. But from each defeat came the living embers to feed the fires of resistance yet to be. That plaster copy of a Roman marble, copy of a Greek bronze from Anatolia, in some way was a *signum* for me of much that I had not yet more than a very shadowy knowledge of; but years later the facts gave substance to the shadows.[75]

Jones's essay on the Dying Gaul was chosen as the title of his second, posthumous collection of papers by its editor, Harman Grisewood; and Grisewood explains his sense of the centrality of this essay by claiming that 'Wales' in Jones's work acts as a particular, localised image of a more general truth. In the encounter between 'Rome' and 'Wales' in Jones's later poetry, Grisewood says,

'Rome' is not only the historic Rome. It is also the large, conquering, imperial power of money or of military might, wherever in history it is found. And though his devotion to Wales was indeed real and heartfelt, 'Wales' is not only the British Principality but is also any small, self-conscious, oppressed and oppositional, historic group. That encounter and its consequences are in David's work as actual and significant for today and tomorrow as they were when the Gauls climbed the Tarpeian Rock, or when Llewelyn the Last was murdered in the woods at Builth.[76]

And, generalising from this, Grisewood thinks that Jones's 'keenest sympathies were with defeat, and with the efforts of the defeated to survive. Achilles was never a hero to David. His heart was with Hector in the dust.'[77]

The conflict between Rome and Wales is not fully articulated until Jones's later poetry (although it is always well to remind ourselves that some of the poetry eventually collected in *The Sleeping Lord and Other Fragments* was written before, and during, composition of the material that eventually became *The Anathemata*. I discuss this further in my next chapter). Nevertheless, this comment is helpfully suggestive in considering the Welsh material in *The Anathemata*, where Jones wishes to convey precisely this sense of Wales as 'oppressed' by, and 'oppositional' to, not only a more uniform and imposed colonial or imperial culture ('Rome' in the later work), but also to a modern civilisation in decadence and decay, characterised by the Arthurian 'Pellam's land' of the opening of 'Rite and Fore-Time' and the poem's associated strain of waste land imagery. This resistance to oppression, this pull of opposition, provides, I think, the essential imaginative energy of the work. The Celtic tradition is being celebrated in *The Anathemata* in assertive defiance of cultural uniformity: its attenuated meanings and significances are being newly *compelled* into recognition through Jones's heroic effort. And the strain that inevitably accompanies this compulsion is basic to an understanding of the kind of relationship Jones has to this, his major, cultural 'sign'.

For it is obvious that not every reader will be able to grant the degree of recognition to the significance of these deposits that Jones works for himself. But what Jones's use of his material can compel is recognition—at least at the imaginative level demanded by the poem—for the view of the historical process which it enacts. In David Jones's work, the Celtic tradition embodies exactly his sense of what 'history' is. For all his attempt to renew the validity of its signs, he is aware that, in certain essential ways, the Welsh deposits constitute a 'virtually lost tradition'. And not only are they now 'lost' to general consciousness, but they themselves speak about, and attempt to come to terms with, exactly this sense of loss; they present, 'The Dying Gaul' insists, 'a kind of defeat-tradition' in which 'the Gaul dies daily'.[78] The tradition of the Celts is important, poetically, to David Jones not only because it is his own inheritance, but because it is articulate about the possibility of its own extinction and because, within that very act of articulation, it bears witness to an heroic effort at survival.

To be articulate in this way is, for David Jones, to be articulate about history itself; and it is in this sense that *The Anathemata* might be thought to fulfil the Poundian requirement of epic: it is 'a poem including history'.[79] The Celts lament their lost battles, their confiscated territorial rights, their slain leaders; and we of the modern diaspora lose all sense of identification with a territory in 'the placeless cosmopolis of the technocrats' for, in our time, 'the genii and *numina* of place "troop to th'infernall jail" in a way Milton never saw.'[80] The savage vanquishing of the magnificent culture of the Incas is seen in 'Art in Relation to War' as 'a glaring example of something which is ubiquitous and universal and which is happening all the time in many millions of lesser ways—to lesser perfections of all kinds; it is in fact, history, your history and my history no less than world history.'[81] In his sequence actually called *History,* Robert Lowell writes memorably in the early poem, 'Our Fathers', that 'we lack staying power, though we will to live.' And if history, for David Jones, *is* loss, it is also a stubborn will towards keeping, hoarding, re-discovering, conserving. His self-conscious re-presentation of his Celtic inheritance, with the struggle and strain and difficulty of articulation that this involves in *The Anathemata*, is the ultimate witness to, and expression of, his view of history. David Jones knows in his own blood the pain of losing a tradition; and his very lack of inwardness with his *materia poetica* in his own poem is the deepest possible expression of the poem's central sense of what it is to lose a true culture. Jones recognises his own lack and limitation, but refuses to admit that this is sufficient reason for abandoning the use of this material in his work. Thus, the painful labour apparent in his use of the Welsh deposits and language in *The Anathemata* manifests a pessimism informed and transformed by a resilient refusal to capitulate.

But this quality of resilient pessimism, or pessimistic resilience, characteristic of Jones's work, is the result also of his sense that if man 'can at best suffer the circumstances of his nativity and tradition', he nevertheless 'can, must, and does, make a song about it.'[82] It is this joy of making a song about it, a song of deeds, that most often restrains David Jones's work from elegy and lament. Such joy is no vague, 'romantic' subjectivism, but a belief that the artist partakes through his 'making' in that gratuitous creation that sustains the world in being. In Jones's theology, the world is gratuitously made by God; and the artist imitates this creativity in his own works. Eric Gill, in a way Jones would surely have appreciated, sees the Incarnation itself as 'a work of art, a thing *made*';[83] and certainly the Incarnation is, for David Jones, the primary human and religious fact—the supreme fact, not the supreme fiction. Jones's Catholicism provides assurance for him that if human history, as far as we can see, is irreparable loss, the Incarnation has penetrated history and made it meaningful:

> For all WHOLE WORKS FOLLOW THEM
>   among any of these or them
> *dona eis requiem.*
>   (He would lose, not any one
>   from among them.
> Of all those given him
>   he would lose none.)
>
>   (*Ana*, 65)

The artist, then, enters into a continuity of 'incarnation' in his work which earns its value from the divine Incarnation which it imitates. 'There is no escape from incarnation', says Jones in 'Religion and the Muses': 'it's like a shunting train.'[84] Hence in his work, whatever the elegiac sense of history's defeats, the world itself is always *there,* redeemed and to be wondered at. When, in 'James Joyce's Dublin', he calls Joyce 'the most incarnational of artists', he means that Joyce has the ability, supremely, 'to make the universal shine out from the particular.'[85] As the body which Christ 'entered' revealed the glory of the Creator, the artist's works must hold up incarnate signs of universal meaning. Hence Jones's insistence on the intransigent facts of the world's existence. The imagination proceeds 'from the known to the unknown'[86] and must never act, as it were, like a colonialist or an imperialist in relation to reality, but must always allow *things* their quiddity and autonomy:

> The concrete, the exact dimensions, the contactual, the visual, the bodily, what the senses register, the assembled data first—*then* is the "imagination" freed to get on with the job. The vague, the fanciful, the generalized have no place.[87]

This applies to all the transformations of reality in David Jones's work—to geology, geography, history, religion, seafaring and all crafts and trades, and to language itself. The patient scholarship of his work, the desire to 'get it right', is the result of his belief in art as incarnation: the world's body can be transformed only when it is humbly recognised as other and separate and distinct. This recognition of 'otherness' is the source of the transforming joy of *The Anathemata*: the incarnations of art, which turn the world and its interests and objects into 'signa' and 'anathemata', are a redemption from the losses of history. And this, at least, is, for David Jones, permanent in human nature: 'We were then *homo faber, homo sapiens* before Lascaux and we shall be *homo faber, homo sapiens* after the last atomic bomb has fallen.'[88]

This deep sense of involvement in, and contribution to, a tradition of making is the great affirmation to be set against Jones's sense of decline and loss; and it is highly significant that he should refer, in this respect, to Lascaux. In the important essay, 'Use and Sign', he insists that 'Michelangelo is no "better" than but only different from, the Palaeolithic masters, as the caves at Lascaux show';[89] and this Palaeolithic genius of form is celebrated at a climactic moment of *The Anathemata* itself:

> And see how they run, the juxtaposed forms,
> brighting the vaults of Lascaux; how the linear is wedded
> to volume, how they do, within, in an unbloody manner,
> under the forms of brown haematite and black manganese on
> the graved lime-face, what is done, without,
>   far on the windy tundra
> at the kill
> that the kindred may have life.
>
> (*Ana*, 60)

In 'Tradition and the Individual Talent', Eliot describes the changes in what he calls, famously, the 'mind of Europe', not as improvement, but as 'a development which abandons nothing *en route*, which does not superannuate either Shakespeare, or Homer, or the rock drawing of the Magdalenian draughtsmen.'[90] Eliot, in 1919, had actually visited Lascaux and seen the rock drawings there, and his sense of a 'tradition' of artistic creation before which the individual artist must humbly acknowledge his inferiority was no doubt vindicated by the grandeur of this incomprehensibly remote, 'primitive' art form. The 'simultaneous order' of Eliot's tradition, and his whole concept of a coherent 'mind of Europe', are possible in his work despite his equally necessary theory of a 'dissociation of sensibility' in the seventeenth century. For David Jones, even more radically, a sense of continuity with the past—and, particularly, with the remotely distant past—is possible, despite his belief in a nineteenth century 'Break'. In the waste 'Pellam's land' evoked at the beginning of *The Anathemata*, the possibility of discovering lost continuities, of building a Boethian bridge over the chasm of industrialism into a more fertile past, is the one sustaining comfort. The tradition of human creativity, of signs of otherness made by men and lifted up to the gods, provides, David Jones has said, a 'sheet-anchor in times of bewilderment'. That is, he adds, 'at all times'.[91]

Notes

1. Margaret Bottrall (ed.), *William Blake: Songs of Innocence and Experience: A Casebook* (London, 1969), p. 63.
2. ibid., p. 64.
3. 'Epics from Outer Space and Wales', *New York Times Book Review*, 21 July 1963, p. 4.
4. *The Colours of Clarity*, op. cit., p. 116.
5. 'Extract from a letter to Fr. Desmond Chute', *Agenda*, 17 nos. 3-4—18 no. 1, Autumn-Winter-Spring 1979-80, 275.
6. See *Epoch and Artist* (London, 1959; 1973 edn.), p. 46, where Jones is obviously indebted to Hopkins's use of Duns Scotus's 'haecceitas'. All further references to *Epoch and Artist* will be to this 1973 edition, and will be cited *EA*.
7. *EA*, pp. 193-4.
8. ibid., pp. 105, 147.
9. *Ruskin Today* (London, 1964), p. xv.
10. 'Note of Introduction', op. cit., in David Jones, *In Parenthesis* (London, 1937; 1963 edn.), pp. vii-viii. All subsequent references to *In Parenthesis* will be to this 1963 edition and will be cited *IP*.
11. *The Dying Gaul and Other Writings* (London, 1978), p. 129. All subsequent references to this collection will be cited *Gaul*.
12. Peter Levi, 'The Poetry of David Jones', *Agenda*, 5 nos. 1-3, Spring-Summer 1967, 87.
13. *EA*, p. 288.
14. Oswald Spengler, *The Decline of the West* (London, 1932), vol. 1, p. 41. Jones discusses the point in 'Art in Relation to War', *Gaul*, pp. 123-166.
15. *EA*, p. 242.
16. Spengler, vol. I, p. 5.
17. David Jones, *The Anathemata* (London, 1952; 1972 edn.), p. 115. All subsequent references, unless otherwise stated, will be to this edition, and will be cited *Ana* within the body of my text.
18. Spengler, vol. I, p. 148.
19. Cf., among many instances, *EA*, p. 57 and *Ana*, p. 49.
20. *Gaul*, p. 134. Cf. also *The Sleeping Lord and Other Fragments* (London, 1974), p. 64, where the prayer to the Tutelar of the Place is 'In the December of our culture ward somewhere the secret seed.' All subsequent references to this text will be cited *SL*.
21. Cf. *EA*, p. 268 and *Ana*, p. 204.
22. Pontius Pilate as 'the fact-man', *Ana*, 239, is a direct debt to Spengler, vol. II, p. 12.
23. *The Modern Century* (Toronto, 1967), p. 42.
24. *For Continuity* (Cambridge, 1933), p. 139.
25. René Hague (ed.), *Dai Greatcoat: A self-portrait of David Jones in his letters* (London, 1980), p. 115.
26. 'Now and in England', *Spectator*, 4 May 1974, p. 547.
27. *Gaul*, p. 115.
28. 'Aesthetics of Crisis', *New Yorker*, 22 August 1964, p. 114. Jones applauds Rosenberg's review in Ruth Pryor (ed.), *David Jones: Letters to Vernon Watkins* (Cardiff, 1976), p. 77.
29. *EA*, p. 104.

30. 'David Jones and "The Break" ', *Agenda*, 15 nos. 2-3, Summer-Autumn 1977, 126-131. The passage Jones is thought to have had in mind is in Morris's *Hopes and Fears For Art* (London, 1882), p. 82.
31. Cf. Cook and Wedderburn (eds.), *The Works of John Ruskin* (London, 1905), vol. xx and *The Collected Works of William Morris* (London, 1914), vol. xxii.
32. There are accounts of this community in Gill's own *Autobiography* (London, 1940), in Robert Speaight, *The Life of Eric Gill* (London, 1966) and in Donald Attwater, *A Cell of Good Living: The Life, Works and Opinions of Eric Gill* (London, 1969). But the most straightforward account of the ideas which sustained the community is to be found in Walter H. Shewring, *Making and Thinking* (London, 1959).
33. *EA*, p. 183.
34. Gill uses this formulation frequently—with, indeed, an irritating repetitiveness—throughout his essays; but it is in fact borrowed from Ananda Coomaraswamy, *The Transformation of Nature in Art* (London, 1934).
35. Cf. *EA*, p. 149 and *Gaul*, p. 161, where Jones is quoting Gill.
36. *EA*, p. 88.
37. ibid., p. 86.
38. *Gaul*, p. 167.
39. ibid., pp. 173, 178.
40. Translated as *The Philosophy of Art* (Ditching, 1923). René Hague offers testimony of the central significance of Maritain's book in 'A Personal Memoir', *Blackfriars*, xxii, no. 251, February 1941, 91: 'Night after night we studied it, with David Jones and Dom Theodore Bailey, under Eric's sort of presidency.' Cf. Jones's own remarks, *EA*, p. 172.
41. The actual quotations here are from Maritain, op. cit., pp. 13, 81.
42. *Puzzles and Epiphanies* (London, 1962), p. 30.
43. See René Hague, *David Jones* (Cardiff, 1975), p. 56, where he is quoting a letter from Jones.
44. A note in the preface to *The Anathemata*, p. 37, tells us that Jones read the outline of de la Taille's thesis published in 1934, but that he also knew a work based on it, Martin C. D'Arcy's *The Mass and the Redemption* (London, 1926). *The Mystery of Faith: An Outline* was in fact published in London in 1930, and went into a second edition in 1934. David Jones's library, now housed in the National Library of Wales at Aberystwyth, contains a copy of the full text of the 1934 edition of *The Mystery of Faith and Human Opinion Contrasted and Defined*.
45. de la Taille, full text, p. 201.
46. ibid., p. 212.
47. *SL*, p. 36.
48. *EA*, p. 163.
49. ibid., pp. 150, 155.
50. ibid., p. 167.
51. Spengler, op. cit., vol. I, p. 174.
52. *The Shape of the Liturgy* (Westminster, 1945), p. 161. Jones quotes this definition in *Ana*, p. 205, n. 1.
53. *EA*, p. 140.
54. ibid., pp. 140, 141.
55. *The Pound Era* (London, 1972; 1975 edn.), p. 278.
56. *T. S. Eliot's Social Criticism* (London, 1971), p. 97.
57. London, 1933; 1964 edn., p. 22.
58. *Selected Essays* (London, 1931; 1951 edn.), p. 19.

59. Roger Kojecky, for instance, traces the influence of Maritain on Eliot, and the anthropologists W.F.Jackson Knight and Christopher Dawson were influential on both Eliot and Jones, and had personal contact with Jones. Jones also, of course, shared a friendship with Eliot.
60. *The Sense of an Ending* (New York, 1967), p. 112. The most limiting statement of Eliot's concept of 'tradition' occurs in the book he withdrew from publication, *After Strange Gods* (London, 1934), p. 18, where he says that tradition 'involves all those habitual actions, habits and customs, from the most significant religious rite to our conventional way of greeting a stranger, which represent the blood kinship of "the same people living in the same place".' It is not difficult to see how such a view might lead to reactionary extremes and, specifically, to anti-semitism, which nowhere taints David Jones's work.
61. *EA*, p. 289.
62. ibid., p. 88.
63. 'Yr Iaith', *Planet*, 21, January 1974, p. 5.
64. 'Message from Mr. David Jones', a privately circulated, unpublished address to the University of Wales on Jones's acceptance of an honorary D. Litt. in 1960, unpaginated. I am grateful to my colleague, Derek Roper, for supplying me with a copy of this address.
65. See Jones's statement to the Bollingen Foundation, 1959, published as an epigraph to *Gaul*.
66. *Selected Essays*, p. 14.
67. *Notes towards the Definition of Culture* (London, 1948), p. 53.
68. *The Need for Roots* (London, 1952), pp. 15, 41.
69. *Letters to Vernon Watkins*, ed. cit., p. 58.
70. *EA*, p. 204.
71. ibid., p. 56.
72. 'Message from Mr. David Jones', loc. cit. The phrase draws particular intensity from its association, in Catholic theology, with damnation.
73. *Letters to Vernon Watkins*, p. 61.
74. Hague, *Commentary*, op. cit., pp. 149-50.
75. *Gaul*, pp. 26-7.
76. ibid., p. 11.
77. ibid.
78. ibid., p. 53.
79. T. S. Eliot (ed.), *Literary Essays of Ezra Pound* (London, 1954; 1960 edn.), p. 86.
80. *Gaul*, pp. 38, 88.
81. ibid., p. 154.
82. *EA*, p. 241.
83. *Last Essays* (London, 1942), p. 9.
84. *EA*, p. 105.
85. ibid., p. 304.
86. ibid., p. 30.
87. ibid., p. 306.
88. ibid., p. 184.
89. *Gaul*, p. 178.
90. *Selected Essays*, p. 16.
91. A private letter, dated 30 August 1968, quoted in Samuel Rees, *The Achievement of David Jones, Anglo-Welsh Poet*, PhD thesis, University of Washington, 1969, unpublished, pp. 42-3.

CHAPTER II
Alone in Pellam's Land: The Genesis of the Poem

> The cult-man stands alone in Pellam's land:
> more precariously than he knows he guards
> the *signa* . . .
>
> (*Ana*, 50)

In the preface to *The Anathemata* which may, like the notes he appends to the poem, be considered an integral part of the work itself, a kind of 'argument', David Jones stresses the accidental and fragmentary nature of his undertaking:

> Part of my task has been to allow myself to be directed by motifs gathered together from such sources as have by accident been available to me and to make a work out of those mixed data. . . . I regard my book more as a series of fragments, fragmented bits, chance scraps really, of records of things, vestiges of sorts and kinds of *disciplinae*, that have come my way by this channel or that influence.
>
> (*Ana*, 9, 34)

His profound sense of the poem's growth during the course of his ordinary experience and reading, worked and re-worked over a lengthy period (from 1938-1945, in some form, and again 'rewritten intermittently between 1946 and 1951', as the preface tells us) achieves its most direct expression in the extreme tentativeness of his subtitle—'fragments of an attempted writing'—and in the sentence quoted from Nennius with which the preface opens, 'I have made a heap of all that I could find.'

Such a sense of fragmentation in the composition of his work is intimately related to Jones's view of the society out of which that work has grown, and of the artist's place within it, as I have, I hope, made clear in my opening chapter; and this relation of 'form' and 'content', or of form and *meaning*, is one that will be explored later. But it is worth emphasising here that, even after the publication of *The Anathemata*, and in polite opposition to some of its explicators, Jones was insistent on the essentially open nature of his writing. In an extremely valuable letter to Saunders Lewis[2] which fleshes out what is very briefly mentioned in a short paragraph of the preface, he traces the genesis of the poem from a large amount of disparate material, quaintly referred to as his 'wodges of stuff', which he could not bring into any coherent arrangement. Much of this material eventually surfaced, in variously re-organised forms, as some of the separate poems in *The Sleeping Lord and Other Fragments*, a book for the most part very different in character from *The Anathemata*. This difference, which is important in understanding Jones's intention in *The Anathemata*, may best be seen—paradoxically perhaps—by examining the style and texture of a brief passage from that poem which most closely approximates the manner of *The Sleeping Lord* sequence. From Part VIII of *The Anathemata*, 'Sherthursdaye and Venus Day', the passage evokes Pilate sleeping at the time of Christ's crucifixion:

> It is the empty time
> > after tiffin
> and before his first stiff peg.
> The fact-man, Europa's vicar
> the Samnite of the Pontian *gens*
> within the conditioned room
> > sleeps on
> secure under the tiffany.
> > They sting like death
> at afternoon.
>
> > > > (*Ana*, 239)

In its content, this passage is close to the Roman poems in *The Sleeping Lord* in that it deals with a Roman official in Palestine at the time of Christ's death. And, formally, it is close to those poems in its intense, powerful dramatisation, and in its language freighted with active irony. 'Tiffin' and 'tiffany', with restrained economy, force Pilate and the empire he serves into judgmental relation with that other imperial 'robbery' that was Anglo-India.[3] The room is 'conditioned' because the politics and history it houses are dependent on a necessary and severe conjunction of circumstances, created partly by the power of imperial Rome but created also, Jones is implying, by a greater power than that; and the word also presumably glances at 'air-conditioned' and thus reminds us that what happened in this room has a significance in our present. And the final assertion that the pain inflicted by the mosquitoes of Judaea is 'like death' bears an obliquely ironic relationship to the real death occuring at the precise moment when Pilate sleeps 'secure'. These immensely assured strategies of local dramatisation and irony are very close to those of the 'later' Roman poems, and they are so unlike the poetry of most of *The Anathemata* that I can think of only one other passage in the entire poem that works in a comparable way. This is the section from 'Middle-Sea and Lear-Sea' which deals with the 'syndicate's agent' in the time of Tiberius Gracchus and his 'bit from the Urbs' who 'waits in the car' (*Ana*, 89): this passage employs a similar degree of 'realistic' specificity and dramatised historical irony—although its irony is the easier one of anachronism.

The distinction between such strategies and the predominant mode of *The Anathemata* is one which Jones recognised while sifting and sorting, re-aligning and adding to, his 'wodges'. The letter to Lewis makes this clear:

> I think perhaps the main thing was that I saw or felt the necessity of using the material less 'realistically'—less of a 'narrative'—no less 'real' but using the *materia poetica* in such a way as to make the work more evocative and recalling—with more overtones and undertones,—but making the facts speak for themselves as *signa*, no less extensive in their content, but rather more.[4]

'Making the facts speak for themselves as *signa*': *The Anathemata*, then, *is* fragmentary, and is intended to be so. It does not have 'narrative' coherence; it is not intended, apart from the passage I have instanced here, as historically representational or dramatically 'realistic'; it is meant to resonate with meaning rather than to state, or assert, meaning. Its separate pieces and parts are, in the transforming imagination of their juxtaposition, intended to convey the splendour which, as *signa*, they individually possess for Jones. Fragments, as we shall see, certainly shored against ruins, but also instinct with celebration: 'anathemata'.

At a later stage in this book, I shall examine the intimations of plan, design and form which others have found in the poem, describe the modes of organisation which I myself find there, and suggest the necessity of recognising these for a proper understanding of the work. But I think it important to insist, at the outset, that such structural possibilities were discovered only long after the actual composition of individual sections of the poem. Such an insistence seems necessary for two reasons: firstly, because composition by the juxtaposing and patterning of pre-existent fragments is the characteristic mode of organisation in the modern long poem and relates *The Anathemata* closely to the methods and techniques of *The Waste Land*, of Pound's *Cantos*, of William Carlos Williams's *Paterson*, the three best known modernist long poems; and secondly, because a proper appreciation of the fragmentary nature of the composition of *The Anathemata* instructs us in the kind of poem it really is, and in the sorts of meaning it is intended to convey. Jones's method of composition, in other words, both relates *The Anathemata* very publicly to a literary tradition, and grows inevitably out of the very private necessities and compulsions of its unique author. I want now to examine both of these aspects of the composition of the poem—the former very briefly, because I will return to it later—and then to draw some conclusions necessary to my subsequent consideration of the work.

T. S. Eliot was not given to discussing his own work very often but in an interview with Donald Hall for the *Paris Review* he said of *Ash Wednesday* that, 'like 'The Hollow Men', it originated out of separate poems . . . Then gradually I came to see it as a sequence. That's one way in which my mind does seem to have worked throughout the years poetically—doing things separately and then seeing the possibility of fusing them together, altering them, and making a kind of whole of them.'[5] This sense of his own processes of composition was presumably to the forefront of Eliot's mind when he recognised that 'affinity' between himself and Jones and Pound referred to in my previous chapter. The latter's method of composition in the *Cantos* has so frequently been compared to Jones's in *The Anathemata* as to be be virtually a critical cliché. Monroe K. Spears actually makes the comparison in terms wholly favourable to Jones when he writes that 'the *Cantos* become increasingly uneven, eccentric and idiosyncratic; to an increasing extent they seem lacking in awareness of the present and irresponsible intellectually and morally . . . Jones, in contrast, never seems capricious or self-indulgent.'[6]

Whether we allow the force of this judgement or not, what is perfectly plain is that Jones's methods in *The Anathemata* owe nothing *directly* to Pound: he insists, in a letter to René Hague, that 'during the actual writing of *The Anathemata* I deliberately did not read Joyce or Pound or other "contemporary" writers.'[7] The coincidence of Jones's using techniques of what we may call discontinuous form—the poet discovering shape and imposing order only after the composition of large amounts of material—similar to those of Eliot and Pound, is to be ascribed, Jones thinks, to the state of the civilisation in which all wrote, rather than to any direct contact:

> . . . it seems to me inevitable that at certain epochs in history, men of, in some sense, like minds will find similar techniques in response to a given cultural situation. They may never have heard of each other let alone read the other's work.[8]

Eliot's classic statement of the characteristic form taken by the work of his generation occurs in the preface to his translation of St. John Perse's *Anabase*, a translation first published in 1930. It is here that Eliot decides, famously, that Perse's poem manifests an organisation based not on a 'logic of concepts' but on a 'logic of the imagination'. In one of his reviews of *The Anathemata*—he wrote two entirely different pieces on the poem—W. H. Auden cited Perse's poem *Vents* as an analogue; and Jones, writing to

Auden in 1954, after publication of the review, mentions that Eliot's translation of *Anabase* 'made a pretty big impression on me when I read it in 1931.'[9] The central subject of Perse's poem, of people migrating over the surface of the earth in antiquity and establishing dominant cultures and civilisations, bears an obvious resemblance to the preoccupations of the first two parts of *The Anathemata*, 'Rite and Fore-Time' and 'Middle-Sea and Lear-Sea'; and one might well think that Jones's understanding of how to build a long poem is related quite specifically to Eliot's belief in a 'logic of the imagination'.

For Jones, then, as for Eliot and Pound—and, perhaps, for Perse—the artist's response to social breakdown and cultural fragmentation is a refusal to make use of traditional forms of narrative continuity and a 'logic of concepts' which imply historical continuity and cultural coherence, and depend on shared backgrounds and assumptions. It is one of the lessons of Valerie Eliot's edition of the original drafts of *The Waste Land*[10] that Eliot himself was so uncertain of the continued viability of traditional forms that he was partly willing to entrust the final realisation of the poem to another man. And Pound's own comment on the method of the *Cantos* in Canto CXVI, where his earlier certainties have crumbled into a great pathos of tenderness and regret—'I cannot make it cohere'[11]—suggests, most powerfully of all, the inevitability of discontinuous form and fragmentary composition in the modernist aesthetic.

But, throughout his preface, Jones is, I think, using the term 'fragments' in a rather more specialised sense. Louis Bonnerot conveys something of this when he remarks on the almost inevitable archaeological associations that the word has for Jones: he describes Jones's purpose as 'to use *fragments*, under analogical names such as *vestiges*, *deposits*, *strata*, as witnesses of, and connecting links with the past.'[12] This seems slightly to overstate the case: Jones's primary meaning is certainly a literary one—a 'fragment' is, straightforwardly, part of an uncompleted design. Nevertheless, Bonnerot's comment does gesture towards an idea that is of great interpretative value in a discussion of *The Anathemata*: the fragments gathered together in the poem are, all of them, remembrances or recallings of a past whose essential richnesses—and, hence, whose present significance—David Jones wishes to evoke. The basic nature of these fragments is perhaps best conveyed by looking, briefly, at the writing which Jones tells us he considered a 'link of sorts' between *In Parenthesis* and *The Anathemata*, *The Book of Balaam's Ass*.[13]

Taken from a body of material apparently entirely separate from that used for *The Anathemata*, as Jones's prefatory note tells us, this fragment deals with a period of the First World War later than that described in *In Parenthesis*. Although Jones nowhere refers directly to Passchendaele in his text, the actual location of this fragment, which does describe men floundering in 'the dun sea', becomes obvious. As a result of the chaos and desperation of the place and period, the tone of the poem is deeply anguished, and there is an energetic bitterness and horrified savagery about the piece that goes beyond anything in *In Parenthesis*:

> You will observe the golden lily-flowers powdered to drape a million and a half disembowelled yeanlings.
> There's a sight for you that is in our genuine European tradition.[14]

Nevertheless, the language of its opening lines is recognisably akin to that of *In Parenthesis*—dramatic, spoken in character, allusive, with what Seamus Heaney has called 'the dirt of the actual shining in the light of his vision.'[15] The piece constitutes, in the main, an account of an attack in which there are only three survivors; and, again as in *In Parenthesis*, but of course much more briefly, the mens' backgrounds are sketched in for us before we witness their deaths. In the moment of death, they are heard crying out to their various 'gods'—after first crying out on 'that Creature of Water'. (The 'dirt of the actual' is, as we would expect from so incarnational a poet, present here to weigh in the balance with the poem's metaphysic. On the one occasion when I met David Jones, then an old man close to death, he recalled, with great intensity, the appalling pain of men dying beyond help in No-Man's-Land and crying constantly for water.) The 'gods' of the men can be understood only in terms of their origins and, in describing the origins of one of his soldiers, Jones's rhythms and linguistic manner become markedly different from those of the opening section of this fragment and recognisable, rather, as those characteristic of *The Anathemata*. In these lines we can, I think, actually see the 'link' between the earlier and the later book being forged:

> . . . the paid man of fortune Sgt. Michael Mary Gabriel Olav Aumerle from Sord Colum Cille of the dark tribes of the Féni, long, long since intermeddled with the blond wolves in with the surf-break from Nord Meer o'er the faem via mareel'd Zetland & the Orcades, by Out Isles of Abendsee and making south by east through the North Channel for Sud Isles & Mannaw.[16]

What Sgt. Aumerle *is*—an Irishman whose blood mingles the Fenian and the Viking—is here described through the compression and intensification of the long history and the situating geography of a people into a few words of what is no longer modern English idiomatic usage; though it is, precisely, the usage of many passages of *The Anathemata*—a loamy, densely packed language rippling its etymological muscles. Jones employs it here to convey the inner racial, tribal or 'cultural' reality of a man about to die; his tradition, the thing that makes him what he is, is, as it were, spoken for him (as Dai speaks his great Boast in *In Parenthesis*) before he finally surrenders it. In the time of greatest extremity, a man's whole nature cries of what is essentially his.

The point is reinforced in *The Book of Balaam's Ass* in the pages in which Jones records the men's final death-cries. They utter their 'dolorous anaphora' and utter them, as the poem's cockney voice has it, 'according to what breasts had fed them—for rite follows matriarchate when y'r brain-pan's stove in.'[17] The essential continuity of concern in Jones's work may be established by comparing this with a passage from the introductory section of *The Tutelar of the Place*, one of Jones's most lyrical statements of this abiding obsession:

> Tellus of the myriad names answers to but one name: From this tump she answers Jac o' the Tump only if he call Great-Jill-of-the-tump-that-bare-me, not if he cry by some new fangle moder of far gentes over the flud, fer-goddes name from anaphora of far folk wont woo her; she's a rare one for locality.[18]

Locality: the associations that accrue to a place of origin, uttered in simple, fragmentary recallings, *signa*, are, in *The Book of Balaam's Ass*, 'Gwenfrewi' or 'Aunt Birch' as easily as they are 'the Lamb because he was slain' or 'the Son of Man because he could not carry the cross-beam of his stauros'. Whatever their provenance—the simply and touchingly private or the largely theological and public—such 'fragments' provide redemptive consolation at the point of greatest human crisis. This is, I take it, the meaning of a work which reveals David Jones for the first time using techniques characteristic of *The Anathemata*. What his soldiers here in fact utter are the only 'fragments' left to them of a tradition all too literally in ruins.

The Book of Balaam's Ass, then, a transitional work, would seem to have been intended as a poem in which men become profoundly aware of their origins, of the numinousness of a known and loved *locale*, of what *The Anathemata* calls 'the inward continuities/of the site/of place' (*Ana*, 90) at the very moment when what seems most clearly established by the circumstances of their present history is actually discontinuity, disjunction and non-relation. The 'dolorous anaphora' of these men are ultimate challenges, human and cultural gestures which assert their negations, however hopelessly, of the inhuman circumstances which have condemned them to death. And *The Book of Balaam's Ass* also reminds us that it is the duty of the poet 'while there is breath . . . to bear immemorial witness',[19] to make these cries permanent in art, to act as a rememberer. In this sense, the fragment from *The Book of Balaam's Ass* which Jones himself eventually published may be seen as a microcosm, or a paradigm, of *The Anathemata*. The longer poem takes its origin from the desire to preserve fragments of a known and loved tradition in the face of a crisis which threatens the extinction of that tradition: this is the burden of the poem's preface and has, I hope, in the theoretical terms of my opening chapter, been made sufficiently clear.

But it is necessary, I think, to insist also on the actual, contactual nature of the crisis in the face of which Jones was undertaking his vast act of celebration and preservation. *The Anathemata*, its preface tells us, 'had its beginnings in experiments made from time to time between 1938 and 1945'—while, that is, Europe was once again undergoing the disruption and anguish of a world war. Jones had, of course, participated as a private soldier in the First World War and had written his first great poem, *In Parenthesis*, out of that experience. Now, living in London as a civilian, he had to endure the prolonged agony of the Second. The letters from this period collected in *Dai Greatcoat* confirm one's sense of Jones's deep anxiety during these years. Although the war is directly referred to only once in *The Anathemata*, it is referred to there in lines of an almost despairing, dignified sadness that conclude the section dealing with the 'idea' of England, 'Angle-Land':

> (O Balin O Balan!
>   how blood you both
> the *Brudersee*
>   toward the last pháse
> of our dear West.)
>
>   (*Ana*, 115)

The pathos of the writing here grows out of Jones's haunting use of the story of the brothers Balin and Balan who, in Book II of Malory, 'each slew other unknown', as an analogue of 'the fratricides/of the latter day' (*Ana*, 115); and out of his sudden slide into the language—or *almost* the language, for *Brudersee* is a Jonesian neologism—of the 'enemy' who is also, racially, a 'brother'. The fact that it is, almost inevitably, Malory to whom Jones refers at this climactic moment is itself profoundly revealing. As Nicolas Jacobs has observed, the affinity between Malory and Jones is that 'each is in his way concerned with saving what he can from the wreckage of a particular cultural tradition.'[20] And there is an added pathos in the reference for a reader acquainted with *In Parenthesis* who will inevitably recall 'the sweet brothers Balin and Balan/embraced beneath their single monument' towards the terrible climax of Part 7 of that poem.[21] The way in which Jones makes the war familial at this point of *The Anathemata*, reinforcing our sense of futility and tragedy, and then juxtaposes this with another reference to his constant preoccupation, 'the last phase' of the West, makes the essential point I wish to emphasise here. The Second World War was the *proximate* crisis—as immediate to Jones suffering German air-raids in London as the debauched 'sweet sister death' was to the men of Part 7 of *In Parenthesis*, as the 'Big Willie' trench mortar of *The Book of Balaam's Ass* was to the British soldiers dying in the Passchendaele mud—just as the issues raised in my first chapter were the *remote* crisis, which called forth the 'ultimate challenge', the 'human and cultural gesture' of *The Anathemata* itself, which insists its negation of the inhumanities evident in wartime London.

My sense of *The Anathemata* as, at least in part, a response to the war is significantly reinforced not only by the military metaphors which Jones uses constantly, almost as second nature, but by several further, more oblique references to the actual conditions of the time. At the opening of Part VII, 'Mabinog's Liturgy', Jones sets Neville Chamberlain firmly in his place, without actually naming him, by incorporating his famous 'Peace in Our Time' pronouncement into an account of the 13 BC commemoration, in Rome, of the conclusion of war in the west. Jones's note to this passage is laconic, but very knowing, and, in its quiet, grim irony, profoundly revealing of the quality of English feeling during the first months of the war: 'There have been Temples of Peace built in our time also.' (*Ana*, 186)[22] It seems worth noting too—though I do not myself make much of this—that Richard Ellmann and Robert O'Clair have detected, in Jones's lines on Poseidon in 'Angle-Land', a reference to Churchill's appointment in 1941 as Lord Warden of the Cinque Ports and, in the 'lifted palm' of the same section, a reference to Mussolini's fascist salute.[23]

But the fact that we are intended to think of *The Anathemata* as, in a real sense, Jones's measured response to the Second World War, as *In Parenthesis* was his response to the First, is signalled, I think, by the lines which I have used as epigraph to this chapter. The 'cult-man', the poem's priest/artist figure, 'stands alone in Pellam's land'. The reference is, again, to Malory, and to the land laid waste by the 'dolorouse stroke' inflicted by Balin on King Pellam. David Jones has used this allusion before in his work with very specific application indeed: Part 4 of *In Parenthesis*, in which the men discover, for the first time, the full reality of life in the trenches, is entitled 'King Pellam's Launde', and the reference is taken up in that section by the representative soldier, Dai:

> I was the spear in Balin's hand
>   that made waste King Pellam's land.[24]

It seems impossible that, in the Pellam reference at the opening of *The Anathemata*, Jones is not specifying, a little more closely than is usually thought, the 'land' in question. A London devastated by air-raids must, at the very least, have called again to the mind of this veteran of 1914-18 the conditions of life on the Western Front; and, if this is indeed the case, the restorative celebration of London represented by Part V, 'The Lady of the Pool', assumes a special poignancy.

This point does seem worth emphasising, since *The Anathemata* is often presented, even (perhaps *particularly*) by its most enthusiastic apologists, as a work of formidably arcane and esoteric interests. It is, of course, in certain respects, a difficult and resistant poem; but it does have its origin here, in contemporary political fact. And, in this sense, it helps to provide a context for its ambition and for the measure of its concern if we consider it alongside those other civilian poetic responses to life during the war years, Eliot's final three *Quartets*, especially *Little Gidding*, Pound's *Pisan Cantos* and the lesser, but interesting, *Trilogy* of H.D.[25] Different as they are, all of these large poems make it part of their effort to take stock of what can be saved from chaos: all are, in essential respects, acts of preservation and assertions of the permanent value and strength of a tradition made in a time of human crisis and extremity. Pound's stance in Canto LXXVI—

> As a lone ant from a broken ant-hill
> from the wreckage of Europe, ego scriptor—

is the stance assumed by David Jones also, opening *The Anathemata* as the 'cult-man' who stands 'alone in Pellam's land', precariously guarding the *signa*. And Pound's famous hope in Canto LXXXI, 'To have gathered from the air a live tradition/or from a fine old eye the unconquered flame', may suggest also the scope of the desire implicit in *The Anathemata*. And the cult-man of Jones's poem stands alone, in its opening lines, in a church which may well be situated in the next parish to that occupied by Eliot towards the close of *Little Gidding*, where the apocalyptic pentecostal fires of the descending air-raid doves compel his meditation on history:

> A people without history
> Is not redeemed from time, for history is a pattern
> Of timeless moments. So, while the light fails
> On a winter's afternoon, in a secluded chapel
> History is now and England.

The Anathemata could be regarded as a drawing out by David Jones of the full implications of how, precisely, for him, 'history is now and England'. With such a context in mind, one may not be going too far in claiming, indeed, that if *In Parenthesis* is not, as Jones insists in his preface, a 'war book', then perhaps *The Anathemata* is.

There is one further point to be made before concluding these introductory remarks on the origins of the poem. It is a point which may, again, be focussed through my epigraph. The 'cult-man' in these lines is, deliberately, an impersonal and unindividuated figure, the contemporary inheritor of a tradition of religious and artistic cult-making, or culture-making, with which the entire poem concerns itself. But the preface leaves us in no doubt that it is David Jones himself, with his own particular inheritance, who preserves and conditions this particular 'cult'. The point is so basic as hardly to bear the making of it, were it not for the fact that it has been widely ignored or misunderstood. The preface instructs us in it quite clearly when Jones discusses the 'biographical accidents' which 'are responsible for most of the content and have had an overruling effect upon the form of this writing.' 'One is trying', he writes, 'to make a shape out of the very things of which one is onself made':

> So that to the question: What is this writing about? I answer that it is about one's own 'thing', which *res* is unavoidably part and parcel of the Western Christian *res*, as inherited by a person whose perceptions are totally conditioned and limited by and dependent upon his being indigenous to this island. In this it is necessarily insular; within which insularity there are the further conditionings contingent upon his being a Londoner, of Welsh and English parentage, of Protestant upbringing, of Catholic subscription.
>
> [Hence . . .] certain words, terms and occasionally phrases from the Welsh and Latin languages and a great many concepts and motifs of Welsh and Romanic provenance have become part of the writer's *Realien*, within a kind of Cockney setting.
>
> <div align="right">(<i>Ana</i>, 11)</div>

This clearly implies that the realities confronted by *The Anathemata*, and the way in which they are confronted, are extremely personal and individual, the unique *Realien*, 'accidentally', of this unique man, David Jones. Jones's desire to make this as clear as possible extends to the lettering he designed for the dust-jacket of the poem's hardback edition (very badly reproduced on the front cover of the paperback) which actually entitles the work 'David Jones' Anathemata' and, in the omission of the definite article, asserts a more pronounced possessive relationship between the poem's commemorated facts and their commemorator: this poem *is* what 'David Jones' has to commemorate and celebrate, to 'make over to the gods'.

This sense of the poem as personal testament is apparent also in Jones's choice of a quotation from the *Dies Irae*, 'Teste David cum Sibylla', as an epigraph immediately preceding 'Rite and Fore-Time'. This not only points to the intimate relationship between pagan and Christian mysteries which it is part of the poem's meaning to assert, but also, in using its author's Christian name, 'signs' the poem in something of the way in which David Jones sometimes signs his paintings, using only his Christian name and the initial of his surname—'David J.' This is also, understandably, the way David Jones signs many of his letters; but a letter, of course, is an essentially private communication. Signing oneself so in public is, in a certain sense, not signing oneself at all: a painting by 'David J' or 'Dafydd J' is, without a context, verging on anonymity. It seems to me that, signing himself so, David Jones is signalling the essential privacy of a work that he has to compel himself to send into the public world (we know, of course, that he flatly refused to part with some of his paintings, even when in financial difficulty). And, further than this, such a signature acts as a sort of 'David me fecit' (a *'fecit*-mark', in fact, as *The Anathemata* itself has it) in the early Renaissance manner; it seems to point up that childlike delight in his own creativity which is a large part of the pleasure of a David Jones canvas.[26] I would argue that the dustcover inscription, and the *Dies Irae* epigraph, sign *The Anathemata* in a similar way; they suggest the communication of a privacy, the bringing into public light of a very personal hoard of treasure, and a bright-eyed wonder at his own capacity for invention (which is, etymologically, a *finding* as well as a *making*).

The combination of biographical accidents that formed this man—the combination of Welshman and Cockney, of Catholic and Protestant—may also be seen as, in some sense, *representative*, and this representativeness is a necessary part of the poem's meaning. But this must not blind us to the fact that the 'fragments' lovingly collected in *The Anathemata* are collected and preserved not out of a gratuitous antiquarian interest, and not only out of the impersonal desire to hold again together between the covers of a book, 'for however brief a time and in whatever wilderness',[27] what can no longer be held together in the world outside the book, but simply because they are the known and loved things that make a stay against confusion for this particular human being and artist. As such, they shape a human consolation in the face of great suffering.

And it is important here to insist that Jones is quite specific about a source of crisis and extremity even more proximate than that of the war. In the letter to Saunders Lewis which I have already cited, he states that in 1947 he suffered a return of the nervous breakdown which he had already undergone in 1932; and, indeed, in the preface to *The Anathemata* itself, he thanks those doctors and nurses 'who, by the practice of their arts, aided me to re-continue the practice of mine.' (*Ana*, 39) It was after the first of these breakdowns that Jones made the recuperative journey, in 1934, that he goes on to describe in this letter. He went to Cairo by sea to stay with

Ralf and Manya Harari (who was later, with Max Hayward, to translate *Doctor Zhivago* into English).[28] From Cairo he travelled, via Lydda, to Jerusalem where Eric Gill was at work on sculptures for the Hebrew Library. In this letter David Jones himself sets such a premium on his trip to Jerusalem that the passage dealing with it needs to be quoted in full:

> The sea-trip had done me a great deal of good, but I was still not up to much and hardly moved out of the Holy City, but used to watch from my window which faced south, with the Mount of Olives on my left and east, and 'the Mosque of Omar' in the middle distance and the tangle of meandering streets from immediately below and stretching away to the west; and I used also to meander about in the densely crowded and incredibly noisy streets and the Suq—chaps on donkeys or mules—Palestinian Arabs in ceaseless argument over the price of anything & everything from a melon to a tin kettle—(the colour of brass but seemingly most skillfully contrived out of discarded petrol-tins)—then suddenly I caught sight of a figure who carried me back a couple of decades or thereabouts, the very familiar stance of the figure, rather bored, indifferent glance toward a closely grouped fiercely gesticulating half-dozen Palestinians.
>
> Or, may be, one chanced to come close upon a couple off-duty: "Gotta gasper, mate? . . . Thanks, what a sod of a place". It might have been a rain-soaked Givenchy duck-board track-way instead of a sweltering Hierosolyma by-street.
>
> But occasionally I saw either from my window or in mouching around, a squad of these figures that secn singly evoked comparisons of twenty years back, in the Nord or the Pas de Calais or the Somme. But now in their full parade rig, the light khaki drill shirts, the bronzed arms bare from above the elbow to the wrist and pale khaki shorts leaving the equally bronzed legs bare from above the knee to the brief ankle socks, the feet in heavy field-service hob-nailed boots, but above all the riot-shields aligned to cover the left side and in each right fist the half-grip of a stout baton, evoked not the familiar things of less than two decades back, but rather of two millennia close on, and the ring of the hob-nailed service-boots on the stone sets and the sharp commands,—so they were a section from the Antonia, up for duties in Hierosolyma after all!
>
> And as the days and weeks passed this analogy I would say increased, but became established—there was a good deal else to think on. I did go to Bethlehem, which is, or *then was*, very beautiful.
>
> What all this rigmarole amounts to is no more than to say that not only *The Anathemata*, but best part of all the various separate 'pieces', such as *The Wall*, *The Tribune's Visitation*, *The Fatigue*, and in an oblique way *The Dream of Pte Clitus* derive from my forced visit to Jerusalem in

1934. 'Forced' because of illness, for it is certain I should never have gone to Palestine off my own bat, for I hate what our American friends call 'going places'.[29]

The opening of *The Anathemata*, which sets the disciples Peter and John 'toiling the dry meander'—'through the byes/under the low porch/up the turning stairs/to the high nave' (*Ana,* 52)—is an obvious reminiscence of Jones's visit to Jerusalem and its 'tangle of meandering streets'; but the whole of this letter to Lewis shows the present becoming, in Jones's historicising imagination, transparent to the past, and summons, with extraordinary particularity and vividness, the presence of the past—the proximate past of his experience in the First World War and the remote past of the Roman *imperium*—into the present. It is as though Jerusalem became, for David Jones, because of its Judaeo-Christian and Roman-imperial associations, a living embodiment of Eliot's 'historical sense'. Jones's recovery of history vibrant and fecund in the Palestinian soil was, no doubt, intensified for a man who really did not enjoy 'going places' and who actually went to very few places indeed for the rest of his life. The fact that memories of this journey open *The Anathemata* should alert us to its importance in David Jones's life as a spur and inspiration to that process of making the present transparent to its past that the whole poem represents.

But the letter to Lewis also reminds us of David Jones's characteristic *stance* as poet-historiographer: even in Jerusalem, much of his observation was done 'from my window'. Many of Jones's best-known mid-period water-colours are, similarly, landscapes or seascapes seen through a window, or 'still lifes' in front of a window (which are never, actually, in David Jones, all that 'still'). This sense of boundary, of a world contained behind its window, opening onto what is outside but protecting what is inside is, I think, as important in understanding the procedures of *The Anathemata* as it is obvious in the paintings. Experience in *The Anathemata* is experience meditated at great length, and in great depth, in a secluded privacy. This is something Jones actually characterises as a 'peculiarity' of his own imagination: 'things, maybe happening or places or things said, hardly register at the time, but rather like projectiles that penetrate the earth but are fused to explode some time after, so things I've chanced to experience or gaze upon don't usually move me at the time, but sometime afterwards, I find, continuously occupy my thoughts.'[30]

This seclusion in a room behind a window was also, of course, a much more obvious 'peculiarity' of David Jones's actual biography: partly as a result of the breakdown he describes in this letter to Lewis and, more obliquely, in the preface to *The Anathemata* (and which are catalogued in some detail in *Dai Greatcoat*), Jones lived a reclusive and, indeed, more or less eremitical existence in the latter part of his life. In any proper consideration of *The Anathemata*, the presence of its intensely solitary writer is, at the very least, a factor to be kept in mind; and something of what Robert Craft felt, witnessing Jones's aloneness during a visit to him with Stravinsky in 1963, should inform a reading of the poem:

> On the return to London, we find ourselves haunted but also lifted by his aloneness. At what point does the self-consciousness of the solitary man—"Sisyphus was a bachelor," Kafka says—and the pedantry, the paranoia, and the overdeveloped sensibilities that are his commonest forms of hypochondria—at what point do they begin to shut him off from the outside? When did David Jones begin to believe in his illness, in other words, and is it agoraphobia, that typological disease of the inward-turning, or is he a *malade imaginaire*? Real or imaginary, is the malady traceable to the war, to experience shared with men that could never afterward be recalled with women, let alone shared with them, therefore resulting in a withdrawal from their society? That great dramatic monologue [sic], *In Parenthesis*, is no withdrawal, in any case, but an affirmation of the world. *The Anathemata*, on the other hand, *is* a retreat, behind language, symbols, obscure reference, and the windowpanes of his room; and it is, to me, a breakdown in communication just as *Finnegans Wake* was after *Ulysses*.[31]

Craft's sensitive questions about Jones's condition—a sensitivity arising from an acute awareness that, despite Jones's troubles, he nevertheless 'attained a life of purity, while my life is one of pastiche'—provides a thumbnail psychology which, however interesting, cannot be pursued here. His judgement of *The Anathemata*, on the other hand, must be taken up again: it is a judgement, phrased here at its simplest, made in varyingly sophisticated ways by some of the poem's severest critics.[32]

At this point, however, I quote Craft at some length merely to indicate how *necessary* a basis in biography *The Anathemata* has, despite the fact that the terms in which Jones habitually speaks recall, as we have seen, the theories of poetic impersonality with which we most closely associate T. S. Eliot. Just as we are now learning to read Eliot as more 'personal' a poet than we have done before (however 'invisible' he attempts to make his personality), it seems necessary also to insist on the essentially personal origins of Jones's work. *The Anathemata* is, among other things, the attempt of a very solitary man threatened by mental breakdown, to endow a lonely life with a sense of meaning and order, and precariously to preserve an identity against an interior pull towards disintegration. In this context, it is worth noting the force of David Shayer's remark that '*The Anathemata* is a beautifully organised but entirely private world; its content offers no answers to our present cultural fragmentation but shows how one exceptional man makes sense of his own past and present by his construction of an elaborate but personal spiritual artefact.'[33]

The compulsion behind *The Anathemata*, then, is profoundly dependent on the individual biography, psychology and imagination of the man David Jones. It is, after all, 'neither a history of the Britons nor a history of any sort' (*Ana*, 9), but a *poem*, a creative product of the transforming human imagination of this man in these circumstances: of David Jones, Anglo-Welshman, Roman Catholic convert, suffering what he understands to be the cultural fragmentation of his own particular time; enduring the architectural fragmentation of London and the political fragmentation of Europe during the Second World War; and, throughout his life, facing the possible inner fragmentation of his own psychological being. Against all of this, *The Anathemata* offers its personal testament of wholeness, integration and health. Above the ruins of so much in David Jones's immediate experience, it raises its vast edifice, building, indeed, in the words of that earlier British poet and painter with whom Jones has sometimes been compared, 'a Heaven in Hell's despair'.

Notes

1. That his reading was thought of as 'experience' by Jones in exactly the way that the circumstances of his life were is evidenced in an interesting aside in one of his letters: 'I suppose for the "artist" . . . the world of "scholarship" is rather like the world of "nature"—one assimilates and uses what one can.' *Letters to Vernon Watkins*, ed. cit., pp. 20-1.
2. The first of two letters published as 'Saunders Lewis introduces two letters from David Jones', *Agenda*, 11 no. 4-12 no. 1, Autumn-Winter 1973-4, 17-29. Part of the first letter is reprinted in *Dai Greatcoat*, ed. cit., pp. 56-7.
3. Cf. *Ana*, p. 88, where Rhea Silvia, speaking as a representative of the Italian people, concludes her account of intercourse with Mars, ''T's a great robbery/—is empire.' She is echoing Augustine's *City of God*, IV, 4.
4. Letter to Lewis, p. 20.
5. Kay Dick (ed.), *Writers at Work: The 'Paris Review' Interviews* (Harmondsworth, 1972), p. 122.
6. 'Shapes and Surfaces: David Jones with a Glance at Charles Tomlinson', *Contemporary Literature*, 12 no. 4, Autumn 1971, 419.
7. Cited Hague, *David Jones*, op. cit., p. 40.
8. Quoted from a private letter in Louis Bonnerot, 'James Joyce et David Jones: Contacts et Confrontations', *Etudes Anglaises*, 53, 1974, 240.
9. *Dai Greatcoat*, p. 163.
10. *The Waste Land: A Facsimile and Transcript of the Original Drafts Including the Annotations of Ezra Pound* (London, 1971).
11. *Drafts and Fragments of Cantos CX-CXVII* (London, 1970), p. 26. The statement takes on an added poignance in the light of Pound's translation of *The Women of Trachis* (London 1956; 1969 edn.), p. 66, where he makes what he takes to be the play's 'key phrase' read 'SPLENDOUR,/IT ALL COHERES'.

12. 'David Jones and the Notion of Fragments', *Agenda*, 11 no. 4-12 no. 1, Autumn-Winter 1973-4, 81.
13. Published as a final, supplementary poem in *SL*, pp. 97-111. Jones's descriptive phrase, 'a link of sorts', occurs in his brief prefatory note, p. 97, which also gives 'the 1930's and '40's' as the date of composition. At the time of writing this chapter, I had not had the benefit of consulting the fuller version of this piece published in a collection of Jones's residua, *The Roman Quarry* (ed. Grisewood and Hague, London: Agenda Editions, 1981), but it is obvious, I think, that this version confirms the conclusion I reach here. The reader who wishes to learn more about the actual dates of composition of this material is referred to this edition.
    The title of this poem refers to the story told in *Numbers*, 22-24; and it is interesting, in this context, that Tolstoy uses the same story as an allegory of the true artist who 'wishes to curse and yet he blesses' in his extraordinarily perverse reading of Chekhov's *Darling*. See *What Is Art and Essays on Art*, trans. Aylmer Maude (London, 1975), pp. 323-7.
14. *SL*, p. 100.
15. In a private letter to me of 27 February 1977.
16. *SL*, p. 100.
17. ibid., p. 110.
18. ibid., p. 59.
19. ibid., p. 99.
20. *Notes and Queries*, NS, 20 no. 10, October 1973, 399-400.
21. *IP*, p. 163.
22. The ironies here are particularly worth noting in the light of the sometimes chilling political opinions revealed in some of Jones's letters of this period. René Hague indeed—unfortunately, I think—decided to withhold from publication a letter from Jones to Chamberlain congratulating him on Munich. It is obvious that, by the time he published *The Anathemata*, Jones had revised these opinions in a more humane direction. In this context, it is perhaps worth noting some remarks of Peter Levi's in conversation with me, that Jones's 'right-wingery is more pro-German than anti-social or anti-socialist. He liked Communists.' While this does not at all excuse Jones's 'interest' in Hitler—lasting at least until 1938, it would seem—it may help to see it as the 'interest' of an old soldier of 1914 who did not want, as he expressed it to Levi, to be 'beastly to the Germans'. It must be said that the politics of the letters collected in *Dai Greatcoat* are only rarely less crude and simplistic than this.
23. *The Norton Anthology of Modern Poetry* (New York, 1973), pp. 566, 567.
24. *IP*, p. 79.
25. First published in its entirety by Carcanet Press, Cheadle, 1973.
26. One of his inscriptions, *Gloria in Excelsis* of 1947, *is* actually signed 'DJ fecit'.
27. See *IP*, p. 22.
28. Her name is wrongly given in the issue of *Agenda* containing the Lewis letter as 'Marya Hagari'.
29. Letter to Lewis, pp. 22-4.
30. ibid., p. 24.
31. *Stravinsky, Chronicle of a Friendship 1948-1971* (London, 1972), p. 228.
32. See particularly J. C. F. Littlewood, 'Joyce-Eliot-Tradition', *Scrutiny*, XIX, no. 4, October 1953, 336-40.
33. An untitled review in *Poetry Wales*, 10 no. 1, Summer 1974, 80.

CHAPTER III
Efficacious Signs:
The 'Content' of the Poem

> . . . and by pre-application and for *them*, under modes and patterns altogether theirs, the holy and venerable hands lift up an efficacious sign.
>
> (*Ana*, 49)

To collect together a heap of fragments is not, of course, to make a poem; and certain of Jones's critics have, indeed, responded to *The Anathemata* in something of the way in which, Dr. Johnson tells us, his contemporaries responded to Richard Savage's *The Wanderer*:

> It has been generally objected to *The Wanderer*, that the disposition of the parts is irregular; that the design is obscure, and the plan perplexed; that the images, however beautiful, succeed each other without order; and that the whole performance is not so much a regular fabric, as a heap of shining materials thrown together by accident, which strikes rather with the solemn magnificence of a stupendous ruin, than the elegant grandeur of a finished pile.[1]

A contemporary version of this criticism might well be John Holloway's account of *The Anathemata* which may be considered a succinct definition of the kinds of objection that have sometimes been made. The 'immense elaboration' of the poem, Holloway thinks, reduces to 'one relation repeated over and over, an endless catachresis of *hinted identity*, thrown off from a diffused agitation of particulars, a quasi-free association, a recession and thickness, a trans-finite array of not-plannedness.'[2] He finds in the work 'no deeper architectonic', but mere accretion; and hence *The Anathemata* is read as a test case of the limits of the modernist method.

As we saw in the last chapter, David Jones himself may be thought to lend some support to such a view in his preface to the poem. On the other hand, he also suggests there certain ways in which the work shaped itself after the composition of separate fragments: 'shape', on the analogy of the plastic arts, is the word he constantly uses to define his sense of the poem's form, as it is also his word for the form of *In Parenthesis* ('I have only tried', he tells us in the preface to that poem, 'to make a shape in words'[3]). It is a word that implies order and proportion, a stripping away of the inessential; its opposite is reserved for the enemy which Jones's whole enterprise is fighting, 'the shapeless cosmopolis'. (*Ana,* 26) Art, Jones insists, is 'concerned with the proper integration and perfection of a shape.' (*Ana,* 30) And his own suggestions in the preface about the shape assumed by his poem are several: it is 'about, or around and about, matters of all sorts which, by a kind of quasi-free association, are apt to stir in my mind at any time and as often as not "in the time of the Mass" '; it is circular, or at least 'it returns to its beginning'; and it is 'like a longish conversation between two friends'. His final image for the poem is 'a kind of coat of many colours', and this suggests, I think, the essential unity-within-diversity which all of his other analogies imply.

David Jones regards the processes of artistic creativity, throughout his essays, as a fitting together, a formal articulation; poets are, he says, 'carpenters of song'.[4] And though these various attempts to describe the form taken by his own carpentry in *The Anathemata* are usefully suggestive for a reader beginning the poem, they are hardly definitive or even particularly illuminating. They stop well short of any attempt to pre-empt the necessary work of the poem's readers whose responsibility, and pleasure, it is to feel out the poem's shape for themselves, through and in the completed work. David Jones is his own exegete only in matters of what he considers necessary textual information: in all other respects the poem is his 'mystery' (*Ana,* 33), its form nurtured in the darkness of a sustaining but not necessarily self-aware creative imagination. *The Anathemata,* more than most long poems perhaps, manifests form as process, as discovery, as 'invention'. And various critics, sensing this, have suggested formal patterns in the work which comprehend and embrace certain kinds of apparent formlessness. David Blamires considers the poem's circularity its basic structure. 'There is no clearly conceived centre to the work,' he says, 'or rather, to adapt St. Augustine's definition of the nature of God, the poem is a circle whose centre is everywhere and whose circumference is nowhere.'[5] Jeremy Hooker elaborates this when he describes the poem as 'a circular maze . . . a form which embodies probably the most elaborate enactment of the ritual pattern of initiation in all literature',[6] although he also thinks that the poem establishes its meanings through the three central symbols of stone, water and wood. Gwyn Williams has suggested that the absence of a centred design in old Welsh poetry—which used principles of construction radically different from those of the classical tradition—lies behind *The Anathemata*: its pattern is, essentially, 'inter-weaving'.[7] Complementing, or perhaps complicating, these notions of the poem as circle, as maze, as weaving, have been various attempts to describe it in terms of the other arts. Blamires has thought of it as collage,[8] and Richard Ellmann and Robert O'Clair have referred to its 'spatial as opposed to linear organisation', in which individual parts 'move in a fluctuating montage'.[9] Louis Bonnerot, alternatively, has described the poem as having 'une veritable structure symphonique',[10] and the musical analogy is also made by René Hague[11] and by Jones's friend and correspondent, Desmond Chute.[12]

Such straining for extra-literary analogues indicates how little critical consensus there is yet about the kind of poem *The Anathemata* is. In my next chapter, I shall consider the principles of order, the 'architectonic', that I find at work in it. As a preparation for this, I want to describe in this chapter the character of the poem *as one actually reads it*. Staying close to the text itself, I hope firstly to convey a sense of the actual material David Jones is handling, the 'heap' which he has 'made', the poem's 'matter', those 'efficacious signs' which he is holding up for our attention; but also, in an attempt to clear the ground prior to the real critical act, to indicate something of the way in which that material is being presented to, and apprehended by, the reader: which is already, perhaps, implicitly to consider the problem of 'form' in the poem, which I shall pursue in the next chapter.

* * *

The Anathemata is in eight sections, of widely varying length, the shortest, 'Redriff', occupying a mere three and a half pages of text, the longest, 'The Lady of the Pool', occupying forty-six. The varying length of its separate sections makes for a variety of rhythmic energy and tension in the poetry, with the full, relaxed rhythms of sections such as 'Rite and Fore-Time' and 'The Lady of the Pool' contrasting strongly with the sharp, staccato rhythms of such sections as 'Angle-Land' and 'Redriff'. In what follows, I am describing, essentially, the way such rhythms are built up and sustained, and the sorts of powers of meaning and music which they acquire over the reader.

I Rite and Fore-Time

The opening section of the poem is exactly what its title suggests. Within the setting of a celebration of the mass (the 'rite'), the poem makes a recalling of the geology of the earth on which the mass is being celebrated, and of the pre-history of the human beings who are its celebrators and celebrants. The priest of this mass, referred to only as 'the cult-man', is the supreme exemplar of all human possibilities of sign-making. The sacramental action with the eucharistic bread and wine (themselves the product of human agency) is made possible by a tradition of sign-making which Jones's poetry attempts to discover at work in pre-history, prepared for by geological formations and transformations. His purpose, then, is to show how 'fore-time' finds its fulfilment in this 'rite'; how 'rite' can illuminate 'fore-time' by suggesting the ways in which the essential mark of the human is to be discovered in artistic and religious cult-making in pre-history; and how a pattern is to be discerned in geological process.

Jones's essential manner of showing the transformations of geology as a preparation for human 'making' is, thus, deliberately to 'con-fuse', to draw imaginatively together, the different languages of rite and of fore-time, of religious ritual and of geological process, in order to create a highly-charged linguistic fusion which compacts a complexity of meaning. In this way, the caves of Lascaux present their images in a theological definition of the eucharist's action, 'in an unbloody manner' (*Ana,* 60); the first kindling of fire from stone is celebrated in a phrase from the Easter *Exultet*, '*O vere beata nox!*' (*Ana,* 61); and the dead of pre-history are incorporated into the Christian mystery through the poem's constant echoing of liturgical refrains from the Requiem Mass and the Good Friday liturgy of the Roman church. Geological process is viewed both as making possible, and itself dramatising or enacting, liturgical process. Hence, the central parenthesis on the human significance of mountain and hill sites is provoked by Jones's reference to the 'railed tumulus' of the altar which contains relics of the dead, just as the tumuli or long-barrows of pre-history do. And, in one of the great set-pieces of *The Anathemata,* the beginnings of the ice age are viewed, and heard, as the singing of Nocturns by a cosmic choir:

> The *Vorzeit*-masque is on
> that moves to the cosmic introit.
> *Col canto* the piping for this turn.
> Unmeasured, irregular in stress and interval, of interior rhythm, modal.
>   If tonic and final are fire
> the dominant is ice
>   if fifth the fire
> the cadence ice.
> At these Nocturns the hebdomadary is apt to be vested for five hundred thousand weeks.
> Intunes the Dog:
>   *Benedicite ignis . . .*
> Cantor Notus and Favonius with all their south-asiled numina:
>   *con flora cálida*
>   *mit warmer Fauna*

> The Respond is with the Bear:
>   *Benedicite frigus . . .*
> Super-pellissed, stalled in crystallos, from the gospel-side,
> choir all the boreal schola
>   *mit kalter Flora*
>   *con fauna fría*
>
>   (*Ana*, 63-4)

The confusion of languages in this passage, a foretaste of the macaronic 'bogle-*baragouinage*' later to be sounded in 'Angle-Land', signals the supra-linguistic nature of the events being described here; it suggests how they happen well above, or beyond, the scope of any linguistic competence. But it also reminds us of the importance, *sine qua non*, which such unimaginably distant cosmic disturbances will have for the cultures of the peoples who will, in the course of time, use those languages.

But the way the coming of the ice age is dramatised here may be regarded, centrally, as demonstrating the essential method of the opening section of the poem. Much of the detail in 'Rite and Fore-Time' is taken from a text which David Jones made his own, Christopher Dawson's *The Age of the Gods* (1928), a study of the origins of human culture in prehistoric Europe and the ancient East; and the reader of Dawson's book will recognise Jones's borrowings and revisions. It supplied a wide area of reference, of information, and of suggestion, for Jones's own poetic imagination. But the overall effect of 'Rite and Fore-Time', its impression on the reader, is totally different from that of Dawson's book. Through Jones's extraordinary imaginative confounding of the pre-history found naked in Dawson with the familiar human shape of the Christian liturgy, 'Rite and Fore-Time' manages to do with the vast reaches of 'era, period, epoch, hemera', with 'the palaeo-zoe' and 'the mammal'd Pliocene', with 'the post-Pliocene/both Pleistocene and Recent', and with the neolithic, what no straightforward scholarly account could do. In David Jones's work, the terrifying vastnesses and recessions of historical and geological distance are, as it were, *domesticated*. This poetry of geological transformation retains the power to terrify and to subdue but, by constantly suggesting a direct human relevance, it sees pre-history not as 'trauma' only, but as 'trauma and thauma, both'. (*Ana*, 69) As Nancy Sandars has excellently said, David Jones tells the story of the past 'not as history, but as something we have experienced in our own flesh; it is closer to direct memory than anything else. . . . It is his, and through him, our family story that David Jones is writing down'.[13] It is not for nothing that the first illustration in the book is Jones's dedicatory piece of lettering, 'PARENTIBUS MEIS ET PRIORIBUS EORUM ET OMNIBUS INDIGENIS OMNIS CANDIDAE INSULAE

BRITTONUM GENTIS'. 'Rite and Fore-Time' is, in this sense, a poetry whose primary theme is *parenthood*.

Actual 'parents', or ancestors, are searched for throughout this part of *The Anathemata*. 'We already and first of all discern him making this thing other' is said, in the first line of the poem, primarily of the priest at the mass being celebrated 'at the sagging end and chapter's close' (*Ana*, 49); but it is the object of 'Rite and Fore-Time' to *discern* those other makers in the course of human pre-history who have prepared, in their artistry, for the possibility of this priest's eucharistic action. This is, then, a poetry of discernment, enquiring into formative influence, asking significant questions, discovering, 'among the elk-bones and the breccia', the essential signals of the human:

> Who was he? Who?
> Himself at the cave-mouth
>   the last of the father-figures
>   to take the diriment stroke
>   of the last gigantic leader of
> thick-felled cave-fauna?
>
>   (*Ana*, 66)

The earliest indications of man as 'master-of-plastic' are discovered in the 'Master of the Venus', the maker of the 'Venus of Willendorf', a limestone sculpture of 25,000-20,000 BC which pays tribute to 'the generative and the fruitful and the sustaining' (*Ana*, 60); in the first makers of fire; in the cave-painters of Lascaux; in the earliest potters of post-Palaeolithic cultures; in 'Europe's tundra-*beata*/who of duck's bone had made her needle-case' (*Ana*, 77); in 'the *egregius*/young, toward the prime,/wearing the amulets of ivory and signed with the life-giving ochre'. (*Ana*, 77) All are, for David Jones, instances of the human animal differentiating himself, and herself, from other animals by making signs of otherness. For Jones, as we have seen, it is in this act of sign-making that man releases his essential humanity; and in 'Rite and Fore-Time' we find the first, and perhaps the finest, embodiment in the poetry of *The Anathemata* of its poet's first premiss, that the artist is not a particular kind of man, but that every man is a particular kind of artist.

It is in this 'fact', and in the geological preparation of circumstances in which this can become fact, that 'Rite and Fore-Time' discovers a purpose at work in the universe and in human history. This specifically religious sense is not insisted, but insinuated, when the origins of art are discovered in religious and ritualistic gesture, and when what Jones calls the 'New Light' is discovered informing the processes of geology and the existences of the earliest men:

> And over the submerged dryad-ways
> intensively his ray searches
>   where the alluvium holds
> the polished neoliths
> and where the long mound inhumes
>   his neolithic loves
> or the round-barrow keeps
>   the calcined bones
> of these, his still more modern hallows
>   that handled the pitiless bronze.
>
>   (*Ana*, 80)

In this insinuation, the opening of *The Anathemata* presents as poetry the theological proposition that pre-history has an informing intention, available to human understanding; and such understanding is explicitly associated, at the end of 'Rite and Fore-Time', with the sacramental action which this elaborate preparation has made possible:

> How else from the weathered mantle-rock
> and the dark humus spread
> (where is exacted the night-labour
>   where the essential and labouring worm
> saps micro-workings all the dark day long
>   for his creature of air)
> should his barlies grow
>   who said
> I am your Bread?
>
>   (*Ana*, 82)

This is, one might think, a religious sense expressing itself through the sacramental theology of orthodox Catholicism, but in no sense limited by it; the religious sense of 'Rite and Fore-Time' is a radically incarnational one. This 'New Light' works cooperatively with the material of the universe and of the human universe; this Bread requires the barlies of human cultivation.

These concluding lines of 'Rite and Fore-Time' return us, then, from the poetry of fore-time to the ritual celebration, but with a fuller understanding of the significance of that celebration in David Jones's imagination. A circle has been brought to a close around a wealth and opulence of recovered data instinct with significance. And in this sense—the circular form, the purposeful recovery of a sense of human meaning in the material world—'Rite and Fore-Time' may be seen as a microcosm of *The Anathemata* as a whole.

II Middle-Sea and Lear-Sea

Part II of *The Anathemata* begins the process of situating and defining the cultural identity celebrated by the entire poem. What Jones calls in the preface to *In Parenthesis* the 'genuine tradition of the island of Britain', is here shown at its formation in the 'cradle-sea' of the Mediterranean. Jones interrogatively searches out those moments of Greek and Roman civilisation that most clearly embody and focus the importance of the Graeco-Roman world in the creation of the cultures of modern Western Europe, and the questions he asks create a marvellously vivid sense of a new, dawn world opening out into distinct freshness and energy:

> We begin already to discern our own.
> Are the proto-forms already ours?
> Is that the West-wind on our cheekbones?
>
> (*Ana*, 91)

The significant moments and events recalled here are dated from an unspecified point which gradually insists itself as the time of Christ's passion and death. This manner of presenting material to the reader is pursued throughout this section and taken up again at the opening of Part VII, 'Mabinog's Liturgy', where it culminates in the very precise dating, down to 'about the sixth hour after/the dusk of it' (*Ana*, 193), of Christ's death itself. Such a technique provides, from the very first descriptions in the poem of what has conditioned this culture, a profound sense of its rootedness in the Christian experience, the experience in which *The Anathemata* ultimately comes to rest, and in which David Jones's imagination as a poet, and his belief as a man, are immersed.

This manner in which time is viewed backwards and forwards from the moment of Christ's death imposes on the poem the ghost of a shape familiar to the reader of Jones's other writings. It is reminiscent of that terrifying cloud of nemesis that gathers over the end of *The Fatigue*, for instance, where we witness the process of historical 'accident' that furnishes a detail for the fatigue party responsible for Christ's execution; and it is like the 'dawn crow of dolour' heard 'down the meander and crooked labyrinth of time and maze of history' in *The Kensington Mass*. The dating method of *The Anathemata* imposes a similar, but much larger, recession of perspective, and implies that the centre of meaning in history is to be found where all perspectives recede to a point, the once-and-always of the eucharistic action, done 'after the mode/of what has always been done'. (*Ana*, 243) History, beginning with the foundational things of the Mediterranean, is, as it were, viewed through the perspective of its Christian fulfilment: in the world of *The Anathemata*, indeed, 'there is no escape from incarnation'.

The moments actually located in this way in 'Middle-Sea and Lear-Sea'—located, one might say, as points of particular brightness in a receding dark tunnel of human endeavour (we may remember Pound's 'In the gloom the gold gathers the light against it' when we read this part of *The Anathemata*)—provide pithy, often gnomic, essential histories of the meaning of the Graeco-Roman world. The fall of Troy; the Quadrilateral Plan; the birth of Rome parodied as a ravishing of the vestal Rhea Silvia by Mars, an agricultural deity now become a god of war (the result of their union was the twins Romulus and Remus, legendary founders of Rome); Tiberius Gracchus; the Dorian invasions: all are presented, economically, in vignette form, along with contemplations of the works of art left by these civilisations.

The Romans are evoked in a way directly related to their meaning in the oppositions of Jones's later poetry: they are 'the men with the *groma* . . . the men of rule, whose *religio* is rule . . . the world-orderers . . . the world-syndicate' (*Ana*, 85), an imperialistic, military culture whose ordinance is divinely sanctioned. In the parenthesis describing the 'sacred commerce' of Mars and Rhea Silvia, Jones captures the slightly ludicrous pomposity, but also the threatening energy, of Rome incarnate in Mars; Rhea Silvia asserts the truth that many of the figures from the later poetry are also made aware of, when she quotes (anachronistically, of course) Augustine's *City of God*: 'Though he was of the Clarissimi his aquila over me was robbery./'T's a great robbery/—is empire'. (*Ana*, 88) It is not surprising, then, that the poem's voice can manage of Roman art only 'Yes, great epigraphers, let's grant 'em one perfected aesthetic—and, of course, there's the portrait-busts'. (*Ana*, 89)

The world of Greek culture, in contrast, utters itself with very different effect in the light-hearted rhythms, the vernal dance, of Jones's lines on the *kouroi*, and other examples of Greek sculpture, with which he associates the '*splendor formarum*' of the Middle Ages in France, when 'the Word is made stone':

> Six centuries
>   and the second Spring
> and a new wonder under heaven:
>   man-limb stirs
>   in the god-stones
> and the kouroi
>   are gay and stepping it
> but stanced solemn.
>
>   (*Ana*, 91)

This part of 'Middle Sea and Lear Sea' reaches its climax in a litany of praise to the statue of Athena in the Parthenon and to the huge bronze Athena Promachos, built by Pheidias to shine over Piraeus after the Battle of Marathon. This statue—together with the sixth-century moschophoros ('the Good Calf-herd') and the marble which Jones calls the 'Delectable Koré'—are brought into relationship with Christian and Welsh mythological figures in a way that is to become characteristic of the poem. The calf-bearer is related to Christ as 'pastoral Lord' (*Ana,* 91), the Koré to 'our Gwenhwyfar' who is 'West-Helen' (*Ana,* 92)—a large mythologising gesture which Jones goes a long way towards justifying in his pages on Gwenhwyfar in 'Mabinog's Liturgy'. And the Athena statue is described, in epithets taken from the Roman 'Litany of the Blessed Virgin Mary', as 'tower of ivory' and 'house of gold'. (*Ana,* 94) These suggestions of identity, employed here for the first time, are to become one of the poem's most characteristic ways of establishing its major meanings. I discuss them further in my next chapter.

The latter half of 'Middle-Sea and Lear-Sea' enacts an archetypal sea-voyage setting out from beneath this statue in Piraeus some time between the eighth and the sixth centuries BC, in which the Mediterranean culture is transported to the Island of Britain, the island surrounded by the 'Lear-Sea' of the section's title.[14] This is the first of the sea-voyages which supply the immediate subject-matter of much of *The Anathemata.* These voyages, and especially that described here, are intended as literal accounts of real journeys in which mercantile motives—in this case, the Mediterranean's desire for Cornish tin—lead to the transmission and exchange of culture, 'out of our *mare*/into their *See*'. (*Ana,* 97) David Jones was passionate in his knowledge of the sea and of sailing, as Arthur Giardelli's account of Jones's research for the painting *Trystan ac Essyllt,* of 1962, makes outstandingly clear.[15] The sea and its business are as necessary—as known, factually accurate data—to *The Anathemata,* as the army and its affairs are to *In Parenthesis* and the Roman poems.

As literal description, the account of this voyage is very powerful. Again, it is that surprise, dawn clarity of the awakening of a culture to new possibility that calls forth Jones's most delightedly precise writing:

> And suddenly:
>   the build of us
>   patterns dark the blueing waters
> and shadow-gulls
> perch the shadows of the yards across the starboard
> bow-wave and on the quiet beam water.
>
>   (*Ana,* 95-6)

But this voyage is also suggestively different from an ordinary, literal journey. To say that it acts 'symbolically' would not be strictly accurate, for David Jones is not, in any of the ways we normally understand the term, a 'symbolic' writer. But the sea-voyages of *The Anathemata* do act as 'signs of otherness' in the way in which I have discussed the concept in my opening chapter.

Kenneth Clark has described a painting by David Jones of a vase of flowers on a table. 'Although no exclusively Christian symbol is visible,' he says, 'we at once have the feeling that this is an altar, and that the flowers in some way represent parts of the eucharist . . . none of this is insisted on, and we are far from the closed world of symbolism'.[16] In exactly this way, without any feeling of closed symbolic correspondences, the ship in 'Middle-Sea and Lear-Sea' 'becomes', in a traditional patristic image, the ship of the Church, and the sea-captain who leads this crew 'becomes' a Christ-figure. This sort of 'sign-making' is accomplished by a deliberate obliqueness in characterisation, the sea-captain being very suddenly introduced as 'the caulked old triton of us/. . . pickled, old, pelagios' (*Ana*, 96); but the anonymity is quickly collapsed into a flurry of suggested relationship with:

> look how his ancient knars are
> salted and the wounds of the bitter sea on him.
> He's drained it again [17]
> and again they brim it.
> Is it the Iacchos
> in his duffle jacket
> Ischyros with his sea-boots on?
>
> (*Ana*, 97)

The language here does not insist on any identification; but the wounds, the drinking of wine, and the word 'Ischyros' (used of Christ in the Good Friday liturgy), all in immediate juxtaposition, compel recognition for the 'sign' being established.

It is one of the most interesting characteristics of David Jones's poetry that it can, as in this passage, sustain a perfectly coherent—indeed, a powerfully evocative—literal meaning and, at the same time, suggest, call up, insist a great deal more, without mystification or vague imprecision. The sea-master and his crew are persuasively present in 'Middle-Sea and Lear-Sea'—fearfully praying to their gods for help in a storm; negotiating directions with absolute compass-precision; croaking their sea-shanties; ecstatically greeting their first sight of land—but they are also illuminated by these further significances. The very real journey described here—so real, in fact, that David Jones could supply a detailed map of it to a scholarly enquirer[18]—can also, like the cosmic processes of 'Rite and Fore-Time', turn into an exchange of versicle and response in which the cries of the shipmen are marshalled to a liturgical rhythm, modulating into the rhythms of a sailor's song:

>Close-cowled, in his mast-head stall the solitary cantor
>cups his numbed hand to say his versicle:
>>Lánd afóre the béam to stárb'd
>
>one to twó leagues.
>And, as the ritual is, the respond is:
>>Lánd befóre the béam to stárboard
>
>one to twó leagues.
>>But, from the drenched focsle
>the stifled murmur is what each heart's wry gloss reads:
>>Rock ahead an' shoal to lee
>less nor half a Goidel's league!
>Is it then
>>each brined throat chanties?
>We've made from Ilissus
>>all the way
>matlos of the Maiden
>>all the way
>>all the way
>from Phaléron in the bay
>matlos of the Maiden
>>all the way b' star and day
>>across the *mare*
>>over the *See*
>to go to Dis in Lear's sea
>>matlos of the Maiden
>all for thalassócracy
>all for thalassócracy
>>Maiden help y'r own.
>>>>>(*Ana*, 103-4)

This serves to dramatise very vividly, almost operatically, this encounter between the men of Middle-Sea and the land of Lear-Sea, but the liturgical form also serves to heighten and transform that encounter. The realism of the episode, as the ship attempts to avoid the perils of the Cornish coast, emphasises the human heroism involved in such voyages; the form implies a larger purpose than the mercantile enterprise the seamen understand. This is the double vision through which all of the events of *The Anathemata* are viewed.

The final lines of 'Middle-Sea and Lear-Sea' begin the employment of a technique of interrogation which continues through 'Angle-Land', the opening of 'The Lady of the Pool' and 'Keel, Ram, Stauros', to be taken up again towards the very end of the poem and, indeed, to conclude the whole of *The Anathemata* on a brooding question mark. The function of the technique as it closes 'Middle-Sea and Lear-Sea'—

> Did he berth her?
>   and to schedule?
> by the hoar rock in the drowned wood?
>
> (*Ana*, 108)—

is to remove into the realm of the deliberately uncertain and inconclusive the end-point of this very specifically charted voyage. The real voyage in search of tin is, at its climactic moment, shrouded in 'the squall-mist and the rain' of mystery and 'sign-making' resonance; and, with the continuation of the technique, the centre of *The Anathemata* is made to echo, similarly, with uncertainty, ambiguity, and a sense of the alternative possibilities which the story of the creation of a culture inevitably unfolds.

III Angle-Land

As the interrogative method is established at the opening of 'Angle-Land'—

> Did he strike soundings off Vecta Insula?
>   or was it already the gavelkind *igland?*
>
> (*Ana*, 110)—

it becomes clear that the mid-part of *The Anathemata*, with its relentless barrage of interrogatives, works as a poetry of *enquiry*—searching out, examining, speculating on its own tradition and cultural history. 'Angle-Land' enquires into the progress of an anonymous vessel up to the southern English coast, past the Isle of Wight, then onward around the east coast past Norfolk and out into the North Sea and beyond ('Cronos-*meer*'). The anonymity of the vessel implies a sort of continuity with the voyage which failed, quite, to come to an end at the close of 'Middle-Sea and Lear-Sea'; but it becomes obvious in 'Angle-Land' that, whatever the metaphorical and symbolic continuities, this particular vessel is making its journey long after the Mediterranean voyage described in the previous part. This is, in fact, a journey made as late as the fifth century AD, and the voyage represents the transport to 'Pretani-shore' of the Germanic cultures of the Angles and Saxons. This is, as the voyage of 'Middle-Sea and Lear-Sea' was, a voyage of cultural 'conversion'—chancy, dangerous, intrepid, but resulting in a new configuration of the land and of the language. In 'Angle-Land', the invasions of the Angles and Saxons are witnessed at work in a nexus of agricultural and linguistic alteration:

>   Past where they placed their *ingas*-names
> where they speed the coulter deep
>   in the open Engel fields
> to this day.
>   How many poles
> of their broad Angle hidage
> to the small scattered plots, to the lightly furrowed *erwau*,
> that once did quilt Boudícca's róyal *gwely*?
>
>   (*Ana*, 111)

The way individual words here ('*ingas*', '*erwau*', '*gwely*') are made to carry a freight of cultural significance—dependent for most readers, at least in part, of course, on Jones's annotation—is a measure of the difficulty of this part of *The Anathemata*, perhaps the most obviously 'difficult' stretch of the whole poem. The difficulty is compounded as the ship 'reaches' Norfolk and the poem attempts to situate the state of Britain at the time of the Anglo-Saxon invasions, when the Roman *imperium* was still a memory in the land and on the tongue, but had in fact succeeded to a chaotic *Völkerwanderung* which Jones expresses in a language that is intentionally 'halting, broken, complicated and Babel-like',[19] that 'bogle-*baragouinage*' heard by 'the ancra-man' (an anchorite like Guthlac) in the Fen Country 'at the *Geisterstunde*/on *Calangaeaf* night'—at, that is, the witching-hour on the night of the Winter Calends. There is no disguising the extreme complexity of Jones's language here, and it is certainly true that 'Angle-Land' cannot be read, but can only be re-read. Its mimetic linguistic energy is the product of a desire to situate in language the moment when a world vanishes and another struggles to be born, when a civilisation rots back into the earth which had once nurtured and sustained it:

>   From the *fora*
>   to the forests.
>   Out from *gens Romulum*
>   into the *Weal*-kin
>   *dinas*-man gone *aethwlad*
>   *cives* gone wold-men
>   . . . from Lindum to London
>   bridges broken down.
>   (*Ana*, 113)

The real tensions and strengths of passages like this lie, precisely, in the dramas of etymology which they enact. Here, most vividly of all in *The Anathemata*, the poem's true subject becomes its own mode of discourse, as Jones works toward making every word, in its concrete individuality, attempt what Eliot, in 'The Music of Poetry', thought it possible for poetry at its greatest intensity to do—to insinuate the whole history of a language and culture.

Before the vessel moves away from the Norfolk coast, Jones allows fifth-century Britain a sudden brief glimpse of one of Norfolk's most famous inheritors, Nelson, in the act of achieving his fame at Trafalgar. The moment of Nelson's death is very precisely dated here ('at twenty five minutes after one of the clock'), and the whole passage has the curious effect of reversing the normal pattern of evocation in *The Anathemata*: here, for a brief moment, the past becomes transparent to the future, and it is as if those '13 fathoms' water' have momentarily parted. But if Jones evokes Nelson here as a particular, but perhaps representative type of later English heroism, the end of 'Angle-Land' is a weary insistence on the tragic historical facts that Europe was enduring during its composition, when England˜and Germany—close tribal brothers whose languages have been interchangeable throughout this section—are now, like the Malorian brothers Balin and Balan, fratricidal.

IV Redriff

'Redriff', the shortest section of the poem, is strategically placed at its centre. It consists almost entirely of a speech by Eb Bradshaw, a Thames-side mast- and block-maker whose original was, in fact, David Jones's maternal grandfather. His speech is addressed to the captain of the ship which has, in this section, anchored at Rotherhithe on the Thames, the 'Redriff' of the title. Or, it would be truer to say, has *possibly* anchored there, for the anonymity and 'sign-making' of the voyage continues as we are introduced to 'Redriff' not by statement but by question; and, furthermore, a question now insisting on alternative possibilities:

> Or
>   did he make the estuary?
> was the Cant smiling
>   and the Knock smooth?
> Did our Tidal Father bear him
>   by Lower Hope to Half Reach?
> Did he berth in the Greenland or was she moored
> in the Pool?
> Did he tie up across the water
>   or did she toss at the Surrey shore?
>   (*Ana*, 118)

The captain asks Bradshaw for expeditious repairs to his ship; and Bradshaw's reply, at the very centre of David Jones's poem, celebrates, in precise and particular technical vocabulary, the nature of the trade, or craft, or art, which he practises. In his pugnacious rhythms, Bradshaw asserts the value of true 'making' over-against the sea-captain's mercenary, pragmatic desire for quick, and scamped, repairs. His language breaks open from a rich and strange nineteenth-century speech into a humorous statement of one central meaning of *The Anathemata*:

>   As sure as I was articled, had I the job of mortisin'
> the beams to which was lashed and roved the Fault in all of
> us, I'ld take m' time and set that aspen transom square to
> the Rootless Tree
>   or dash m' buttons!
>   . . . he's got
> till the Day o' Doom
> to sail the bitter seas o' the world!
>
> (Ana, 121)

In an autobiographical essay, David Jones has pointed to the representative nature of Bradshaw's Ruskinian (or Gill-like) sense of organic relationship with his work:

> My grandfather was a master mast- and block-maker, which involved competence in all that belongs to a ship's carpentry. Which float of Norweyan from the mast-pond? Keel-elm for those caps aloft by the hounding? Best Indies lignum vitae to resheave those heavier running-blocks?
>
> 'The virtue of art is to judge'; 'Art is a virtue of the practical intelligence'. Bradshaw knew nothing of these definitions but, unknown to himself, he practised them. By a happy chance Joyce, according to Gogarty, declared boat-building to be comprehended in practical life as 'art', no less than the making of a poem. It was no accident that the bardic poets of Wales called themselves *seiri cerdd*, 'carpenters of song'.[20]

These neo-scholastic definitions of art; this particular reference to Joyce; the bardic definition of poets: all are familiar as points of illustration and argument in Jones's essays. His using them all together in this passage on Bradshaw indicates how much of his own attitude to the 'craft' of artistic representation, in the plastic arts and in poetry alike, is incarnate in this craftsman figure. At this central point in the poem, the almost anonymous craftsman utters the tradition of pride in good workmanship which relates him, as 'man master-of-plastic', to all the other 'makers' of *The Anathemata*. In this sense, the part played by Bradshaw in the plan of the poem is very similar to that played by Dai Greatcoat in Part IV of *In Parenthesis*. There, again at almost the mid-point of the poem, Dai expresses in his Boast the response of the common foot-soldier throughout history to the imposed facts of his existence; and the speech is done with a cockney pride tempered by undercutting ironies:

> I am the Single Horn thrusting
> by night-stream margin
> in Helyon.
>   Cripes-a-mighty-strike-me-stone-cold—you don't say.
>   Where's that birth-mark, young 'un.[21]

In 'Redriff' such ironies are exchanged for a good-natured and entirely self-assured humour; but Eb Bradshaw's assertion of pride in the patient dedication to a craft is as central to the meaning of *The Anathemata*, a poem about makers and making, as Dai's pride in military service is to that of *In Parenthesis*, a poem about 'unmaking'.

With 'Redriff', the first great movement of the poem reaches its climax. We have been shown a culture making itself through the geological transformations of pre-history; through the movements of peoples over the earth's surface; through the development of languages; through the artworks and cult-objects which incarnate and celebrate, and hand on into the future, a tribe's understanding of itself. Now, in Eb Bradshaw, the tradition has reached the point of full articulation in the poem: he expresses in words what all the poem's earlier makers have expressed in silence. And, in doing so, he also expresses what David Jones, in the shape of *The Anathemata* itself, is doing. Eb Bradshaw's patience, care, tenderness, reverence, supply the axis on which the globe of *The Anathemata* turns; and the sections following 'Redriff' are markedly different in character from those preceding it. This distinction could be best characterised, perhaps, by saying that the first half of the poem presents the 'facts' of the culture which is 'ours'; it describes for us the essential conditions without which this culture would be impossible. The second half of the poem examines the ways in which we have understood those facts; it tells again the stories we have told ourselves about our origins and our destinies; it articulates and contemplates our *myths*.

V The Lady of the Pool

'And indeed nothing is easier', says the narrator at the opening of Conrad's *Heart of Darkness*, 'for a man who has, as the phrase goes, "followed the sea" with reverence and affection, than to evoke the great spirit of the past upon the lower reaches of the Thames.' In Part V of *The Anathemata*, perhaps the greatest section of the poem, its *tour-de-force*, Elen Monica, a London lavender seller, gives voice to the 'great spirit of the past' on one of the lower reaches of the Thames, by 'the bend of the river by Rotherhithe and Shadwell' known as the 'Pool of London'. John Holloway has said of this section of the poem that 'it makes one speak of the creation of myth as well as of its re-creation';[22] and certainly Elen Monica incarnates in her ample person what only David Jones, gathering it all together, could describe as 'our collective London myth'. (*Ana*, 168) Apart from the interrogatory opening of the section, which asks whether the sea-captain did in fact encounter the Lady's '*East-Seaxna*-nasal', her cockney accent, and one very brief interjection by the captain later, the whole of 'The Lady of the Pool', the longest section of *The Anathemata*, consists of Elen Monica's direct speech. This speech, and indeed Monica's 'character', are drawn partly from Chaucer's Wife of Bath, partly from Joyce's washerwoman in the 'Anna Livia Plurabelle' section of *Finnegans Wake*. By making his lady a lavender-seller, Jones may well have been subliminally suggesting the relationship with Anna Livia in the etymological connection between 'lavender' and 'launder';[23] but in any case Elen Monica enters into a kind of dialogue with Anna Livia when she 'answers' Anna's 'tell me the sound of the Findhorn's name' with '*this* is the sound of the Findhorn stone'. (*Ana*, 145) Certainly Elen Monica's is, like Anna Livia's, an immensely rich, elaborately layered and textured tongue which perhaps does for cockney in our literature something of what Joyce does, in 'Anna Livia Plurabelle', for Dublinese.

In 'The Lady of the Pool', after the introductory section which serves to set the sea-captain in the reader's place, as addressee of what follows, Monica's monologue moves out from her lavender-cry into an account of the various London churches outside which she plies her trade, and then into a memory of three of her former lovers, an Oxford clerk, a freestone-mason and a Milford boatswain. The tone of Monica's address is a curiously ambivalent one that manages to combine humour, vituperation and a sort of wan regretfulness. In a letter to one of the poem's critics, Jones defines this for us when he says that 'The decay of the year's fall and the coming on of winter are linked in my mind with the introit of the lavender girl on the street. Her cry was of great beauty but was mysteriously sad. I *think* it was the last of the London street-cries to survive'.[24] The period in which the address is spoken is not particularised—very deliberately, as I explain later—but we will, I think, take the proper measure of its mood and atmosphere if we consider it set in what Jones calls, in 'The Viae', 'the pluvial light of Britain'.[25] Through these accounts—of the London churches (in which Jones draws heavily on Stow's *Survey of London* of 1598) and of her lovers—Monica's soliloquy gradually insists its central point. The immense synthesis of material—legendary, mythical, philosophical, theological, literary, artistic, historical, liturgical (an Hamletian display)—which Monica embodies and expresses, has its focus in an attempt to celebrate the sign that is 'London', the sign that is 'woman' and the sign that is the essential mystery of Christianity. It seems to me that in these respects, and in some others, 'The Lady of the Pool' also acts as a mirror-image of the whole of *The Anathemata*; and in what follows I want to define these impressions.

The record of the churches outside which Monica cries her '*introit in a Dirige-time*' (*Ana,* 125) serves to insist that the Christianity she espouses is continuous with something older and darker than Christianity. The Christian churches inherit the functions of the pagan temples which sometimes actually occupied the same sites. Monica sees St. Paul's as the type of such inheritance when she imagines how its site was once sacred to Jupiter, and describes an old ceremony rooted in pagan ritual being enacted in its 'converted' walls:

> At Paul's
> and faiths under Paul
> where
>   so Iuppiter me succour!
> they do garland them with Roman roses and do have stitched on their zoomorphic apparels and vest 'em gay for Artemis.
>   When is brought in her stag to be pierced, when is bowed his meet head between the porch and the altar, when is blowed his sweet death at the great door, on the day before the calends o' Quintilis.
>
>   (*Ana,* 127)

This celebration of London's churches constantly evokes the 'faiths under Paul', and sets Monica's Christianity as the climax and fulfilment of a perennial tradition of religious worship on the city's sacred sites. The airraids which were bombing some of these sites during the Second World War are an unstated presence in this part of the poem, and when Monica's monologue eventually returns, at the end of 'The Lady of the Pool', to a further recounting of the city's churches, the emphasis falls on the father-figures laid to rest in the ground, analogous to the saints' bones kept under Christian altars, to act as preservers and guardians. Monica's emphasis here is perhaps informed as much by the contemporary war-effort as it is by a medieval spirit of place:

>   At each adytum over
> where under the fathering figures rest that do keep us all.
>   So it's fabled

> in Taffy's historias and gests of Brut the Conditor—
> romans o' Belins, 'Wallons an' Wortipors
>   agéd viriles buried under
> that from Lud's clay have ward of us that be his townies—
> and certain THIS BOROUGH WERE NEVER FORCED,
> cap-tin!!
>
>   (*Ana,* 163)

But Monica as spirit of place is a central embodiment of that feeling for the local and particular, and for the ground as the preserver of ancient continuities, that informs the whole of *The Anathemata*: her insistence, like that of the entire poem, is that 'What's under works up' (*Ana,* 164), and that the human effort of discovering the springs and powers of sustenance is a necessary capacity of the imagination. The point is reinforced by Monica's account of her lovers, in which the central focus of their love is vividly evoked—in the Oxford clerk's love of scholastic dispute, particularly of points of Marian theology; in the freestone-mason's awareness of the constant presence of Rome in the foundational mythology of London; and in the seafaring lore and Welsh mythology expressed through Monica's memories of 'the boatswain from Milford, for each circumstance finding antique comparison'. (*Ana,* 149)

In bodying forth the vigour and necessity of this fundamental capacity of the human imagination, Elen Monica incarnates virtually all of what David Jones wishes 'woman' to mean in *The Anathemata*. She is, firstly, a triumphant *survivor*, a woman alone, not emotionally, financially or socially dependent on men; and this independence, while it may well be read as a tacit refusal by David Jones of the conventional male attitudes of his time (a refusal obviously related to the radical sense of himself as a man who would never marry which *Dai Greatcoat* reveals), also has a necessary functional meaning in the poem. Elen Monica as daughter, as lover and (implicitly) as *mother*, embodies tendernesses and reverences which the imperially male elements in the poem would deny: she acts as opposition and subversion. Her name relates her, explicitly in Jones's annotation, to that Flavia Julia Helena, mother of Constantine, whom Jones's note (*Ana,* 131-2) describes at some length. What he says in conclusion about this extraordinary mythological figure could also be said about the Lady of the Pool herself: she represents 'a fusion of typic figures of great splendour and depth: *imperatrix* plus numinous "beauty" plus Holy Woman.' Elen Monica is all of these things, while remaining a very real, sensuous woman ('Enough! let's to terrestrial flesh, or/bid good-night, I thought.'). To the freestone-mason, she is 'Flora Dea', 'the female guardian deity of Rome, essentially oracular and representing the whole female principle' (*Ana,* 132), and 'Augusta', an ancient honorific for London. To the Oxford clerk, she is his Alma Mater. Like the sirens she describes, Elen Monica is a figure 'exhaling distillations of the entire flora/and of WOMANKIND/to the man at the wheel' (*Ana*, 144). And, indeed, when she insists that 'all that is comprised under mermaid is no mirage', she proves the point by transforming herself, in front of the sea-captain's eyes, into a mermaid/Britannia figure with

> a comb of narwhal ivory, a trident
> and a bower anchor —
>   *and* the Tower lion
> nor twisk his lasher.
>
>   (*Ana*, 145)

The astounded response which this piece of amateur dramatics calls forth from the sea-captain (off-stage, or off the page) is greeted by Monica's statement of a principle of temporal confusion echoing the Fool's famous line in *King Lear* which Jones uses as an epigraph to the whole poem ('This prophecie Merlin shall make for I live before his time'):

>   Don't eye *me*, captain
> don't eye *me*, 'tis but a try-out and very much betimes:
> For we live before her time.
>
>   (*Ana*, 146)

Monica is deliberately removing herself from the processes of ordinary human time to place herself 'in the order of signs', in the timelessness, or the eternal co-present, of myth. In this way, she acts as the paradigmatic female figure in the poem: she asserts, defines and incarnates the essential meanings which all its mythologised characters are there to establish; she restores to life and health the 'signa' which her tradition has handed into her custody.

The Lady of the Pool makes this particularly apparent when she re-tells the story of the Incarnation and of the subsequent history of the Church as a voyage-allegory in which 'the skipper of the *Margaron* . . . the master o' the *Mary*', 'overdue a nine month', undergoes various marine troubles and difficulties. (Some of this is actually very funny, as when—in the most Joycean section of this Joycean monologue—the Church's theological controversies are recounted as a sea-battle.) In this strain towards allegory, the voyage described in 'The Lady of the Pool' provides a kind of summary of the method of much of *The Anathemata*, as the religious significance of this graphically recounted voyage is, quite literally, underlined by David Jones:

>   I saw water
> coming from the *right* side, about midships; yet her list were
> heavy to her lade-board
>   and as I looked I saw:
> she were hulled, SEVEN TIMES.
>   (*Ana*, 139)

The references here are, fairly obviously, to one of the wounds of Christ and to the seven sorrows of Mary; and this voyage suggests, in a particularly intense form, the kind of significance to be attached to the larger journeyings in the poem. As the voyage here reaches its climax, Monica's sense of the importance of her tradition allows her one of the great set-pieces of *The Anathemata*, its central passage on the Crucifixion.

Elen Monica, as we have seen, takes her first Christian name from the St. Helen associated with the finding of the wood of the cross—'the Woman through whom Cross and Vexillum become one' (*Ana*, 132)—and her second associates her with maternity (Monica was the mother of Augustine), an association, it has become clear by this stage of her monologue, that is particularly with Mary. In this climactic moment of 'The Lady of the Pool', Monica speaks in accents, cadences and rhythms very different from her customary style: it is as though her ordinary speech patterns here *cradle* the different language of religious contemplation, forming a kind of linguistic *pietà*. It is a moment of luminous intensity in the poem, in which Jones—combining references to the liturgical *Vexilla Regis*, to medieval lyric, to nursery rhyme—revises Eliot's revision of Chaucer and attempts to restore April to its original verdure:

>   On the ste'lyard on the Hill
> weighed against our man-geld
>   between March and April
> when bough begins to yield
>   and West-wood springs new.
> Such was his counting-house
>   whose queen was in her silent parlour
> on that same hill of dolour
>   about the virid month of Averil
> that the poet will call cruel.
>   Such was her bread and honey
> when with his darling Body (of her body)
>   he won Tartary.
> Then was the droughts of March moisted to the root by that
> shower that does all fruit engender — and do constitute what

> they hallow an'chrism these clerks to minister that kings and queens may eat thereof and all poor men besides.
>
> *(Ana,* 157-8)

'You can refute Hegel', said Yeats, 'but not the Saint or the Song of Sixpence';[26] and this passage from *The Anathemata* presents itself not as argument but as conviction.

At the end of 'The Lady of the Pool', Monica's understanding of her tradition here is shown to be instinct with moral significance when we 'overhear' her attempting to save a 'pretty boatswain's boy' from a beating. With this spontaneous, 'maternal' act of sympathy and generosity, the longest section of *The Anathemata* closes in an insistence on the ethical value of Monica's understanding of 'our collective London myth': she is impelled by what Jones calls the 'significant and warm images' of her tradition (*Ana,* 241), into an act of human lovingkindness. In the world of ethics, as in the worlds of aesthetics and metaphysics, 'what's under works up'; and the close of 'The Lady of the Pool' brings dramatically to our attention what is latent in the whole poem, that the conditions of cultural health which *The Anathemata* explores are intimately related to the moral health of the tribe whose traditions these are, and that poems too, poems like *The Anathemata,* must have their final value judged in the world of human action.

VI Keel, Ram, Stauros

'Keel, Ram, Stauros', a relatively short section after the breadth and sweep of 'The Lady of the Pool', is, nevertheless, strategically extremely important in the scheme of *The Anathemata*. It serves, firstly, to bring to a conclusion the voyage begun in 'Middle-Sea and Lear-Sea'; and it does this by resolving the uncertain, tentative, interrogatory method in short, direct, emphatic gestures of completion. The voyage reaches an end where it literally began, in the harbour at Athens; but the way in which, throughout its circular course, it has been far more than a literal voyage, is also insisted here towards its conclusion when the sea-captain's *imitatio Christi* becomes more or less explicit, and the voyage-metaphor, or voyage-allegory, of *The Anathemata* reaches a measured climax and fulfilment:

> Pious, eld, bright-eyed
> > *marinus.*
> Diocesan of us.
> > In the deeps of the drink
> his precious dregs
> > laid up to the gods.

>   Libation darks her sea.
>   He would berth us
>   to schedule.
>   (*Ana*, 182)

The resolution echoes, and deliberately removes the interrogative from, the tentative conclusion of 'Middle-Sea and Lear-Sea' ('Did he berth her?/And to schedule?'); and this arc of *The Anathemata* is brought to its fulfilment.

The section also acts as a fulfilment of some of the mythical strands of the poem's meaning. At the opening of 'Keel, Ram, Stauros' the principle of temporal confusion at work in the whole of *The Anathemata* is made apparent when the bells of London peal out their version of 'Oranges and Lemons':

>   I do not know!
>   I do not know!!
>   I do not know what time is at
>   or whether before or after
>   was it when—
>   but when *is* when?
>   (*Ana*, 170)

Jones is here echoing Joyce's Anna Livia in the compellingly beautiful close to her monologue in *Finnegans Wake*:

> ... every telling has a taling and that's the he and the she of it. Look, look, the dusk is growing! My branches lofty are taking root. And my cold cher's gone ashley. Fieluhr? Filou! What age is at? It saon is late.[27]

This refusal of temporal particularity allows the rest of *The Anathemata* what we will see as its primary technique, an elaborate process of mythical correspondence intended to reveal the Christian mystery as the centre and fulfilment of the 'argosy of mankind'.

In 'Keel, Ram, Stauros', the mythical fulfilment comes in a celebration of one of the three 'permanent symbols' which the poem uncovered in its opening section, 'Rite and Fore-Time', the symbols which Jones discovers in Virgil's description of the palace of Priam (*Aeneid* II, 512-14), 'the stone/the fonted water/the fronded wood'. (*Ana*, 56) All three symbols are celebrated throughout *The Anathemata*, but stone particularly in 'Rite and Fore-Time' itself, water particularly in 'Sherthursdaye and Venus Day', and wood is contemplated in this section of its own, 'Keel, Ram, Stauros'. What Jones means by 'the fronded wood' becomes apparent here in a passage of transition between the voyage itself, as it comes to completion, and the examination of the wood symbol:

> Down
> > far under him
> > the central *arbor*
> > the quivering elm on which our salvation sways.
> > *Baum,* baulk
> > > ridging the straked, dark
> > inverted vaults of her.
>
> *(Ana,* 173)

The primary significance of wood is, then, recorded as the necessary material of human salvation, the 'stauros' upon which Christ was crucified. But the density and recession of the symbol is pursued through its further significations, as 'keel' and as 'ram'.

As 'keel', wood is the material of the ships whose voyages ferry the cargo of cultural exchange throughout history, and throughout David Jones's poem. The language in which it is celebrated is technically precise and evocative; it is a version of what one of William Golding's characters in his novel, *Rites of Passage,* calls 'tarpaulin language'. Yet it too is superimposed on, or watermarked into, a Christian suggestiveness:

> Prone for us
> > buffeted, barnacled
> tholing the sea-shock
> > for us.
> Three-nailed the strakes to you
> > garboard, bends and upwards
> free-board and capping and thole.
>
> *(Ana,* 174)

As 'ram', wood is viewed under its aspect of threat and hostility and violence, the instrument of war. In 'Art and Democracy', Jones quotes Spengler's chilling definition of man as 'a weapon-using carnivore';[28] and in *In Parenthesis* John Ball's rifle is assimilated to this 'mythical' dimension of wood: 'It's the thunder-besom for us/it's the bright bough borne/it's the tensioned yew for a Genoese jammed arbalest.'[29] In *The Anathemata* war is seen, similarly, as a permanent fact of human experience; and, if wood acts as the agent of redemption in 'Keel, Ram, Stauros', it is also, before that, the agent of crucifixion and death, the 'ram': it is both 'pole for the garlands' and 'gibbet'.

But this section of the poem is centred on the importance of wood as 'stauros'. As such, it is seen as a fulfilment of other cult-symbols, Eleusinian and phallic, and it is viewed as the object of veneration in Christian churches, where 'Demos/with crisis in his unnumbered eyes/ importunes counter-wonders'. *(Ana,* 179) At the end of 'Keel, Ram,

Stauros', wood as keel and wood as stauros are brought together and meshed, as it were, to form the structure of the ship which is then allowed its safe return to harbour:

> Hidden wood
> > tree that tabernacles
> the standing trees.
> Lignum for the life of us
> > holy keel.
>
> > > (*Ana*, 180-1)

VII Mabinog's Liturgy

Just as the wood of the cross is set at the centre of a meditation on all human worship in 'Keel, Ram, Stauros', the story of Christ's birth and death is set in a context that establishes it as the fulfilment of earlier mythologies in the final two parts of the poem. 'Mabinog's Liturgy' and 'Sherthursdaye and Venus Day' enact, as it were, a sort of process of conversion or baptism in which legend and myth become 'liturgy'. In both, the ritual is viewed through a specifically Celtic tradition. Hence, the eponymous mabinog of 'Mabinog's Liturgy' is at once Christ as the young child/hero ('maban') whose story, or 'gospel', is being told here on the analogy of the story of the young Peredur or Percival-figure of the *Mabinogion* who, as 'Chief Physician' in later life, 'frees the waters'; and the 'mabinog' is also the poet or maker himself, the 'tyro-bard'. The phrase, 'Mabinog's Liturgy', is, then, a pun implying both Christ's action, which is memorialised and re-enacted afterwards in the Christian liturgy, and the poet's own celebration of those events. The Celtic provenance of this liturgy announces it very strongly as David Jones's own. As *The Tutelar of the Place* has it, 'Tellus of the myriad names answers to but one name', and the one name that David Jones can give her is a Celtic name. If 'she's a rare one for locality', the locality in which David Jones will raise a response from her is a Welsh one. And, as if to emphasise this almost primordial tendency of the imagination, the voice of 'Mabinog's Liturgy' might be thought of as a child's voice. Its predominant spirit is informed by folksong, carol, nursery rhyme and legend:

> But eighteen days to the Maying.
> > They say it's Tuesday's child
> is chose
> this year's Mab o' the Green
> > *mundi Domina*
> or was she Monday's

>   total beauty
> *Stabat* by the Blossom'd Stem?
>
>   (*Ana*, 188)

The Celtic 'name' of this liturgy is dramatically emphasised in a reversion to the dating techniques of earlier parts of the poem, which now situate Christ's birth at a point in relation to the development and transformation of the Celtic world. This establishes the essential mode of perception in these final two parts of *The Anathemata*. 'Mabinog's Liturgy' works by moving in from these large situating gestures (images of the Roman world at its borders transforming the Celtic 'thing') towards very precise historical and geographical evocations of the facts of the Roman *imperium* into which Christ was born. But both the time of fact and the time of myth in which *The Anathemata* has been moving up to this point are now taken up into what we might call the 'time of liturgy' or 'eucharistic time', when the structure of allusion to the Roman liturgy, and particularly to the masses of the Chrismas season, becomes apparent. Facts and myths are presented, finally, as *signa* of redeemed time. Hence, a reference to the gospel of the Epiphany mass combines with a phrase from Lancelot Andrewes to signal the point at which mankind is 'berthed to schedule', the point at which Christ is revealed, within time, to men:

> Our van
>   where *we* come in:
> not our advanced details now, but us and all our baggage.
>
>   (*Ana*, 190)

The moment of Christ's birth is set in immediate juxtaposition with that of his death. 'Where *we* come in' is the point at which what Christ represents, through his birth and death, is established; so that 'Mabinog's Liturgy', while it concentrates on the nativity theme, and uses primarily references to the Christmas liturgy, also meditates on the death which was to prove the theological meaning of Christ's life and in which, for David Jones, the ultimate destiny of 'us and all our baggage' is to be realised.

Calvary, then, is shown inheriting other mythological significances when the poem's voice invites various figures—Chloris, Flora, Sybil, Calypso, Persephone, Nestor—to witness the 'dendrite beauties' of the Crucifixion scene. These 'dendrite beauties' are a Christian realisation of the 'fronding wood' which Jones found in Virgil, and they imply the informing possibility of resurrection. Hence, the centre of 'Mabinog's Liturgy' is occupied by what Jones calls in *Epoch and Artist* the mythical 'world-dance which has for its maypole the gleaming Tree on which the world-ransom was weighed'.[30] That 'creation of myth' John Holloway recognises in 'The

Lady of the Pool' may be thought intensified here when, in an image of great delicacy and persuasion, Jones joins together the worlds of Christian gospel and Homeric myth:

> Martha! stop that endless meddling!
> and don't tie Argos up
>   or, he'll bark
> the place down.
> He's a nose for what springs new
> from hoar stem
>   and ancient holm.
> Let him come gently.
> See! he would reach to lick
>   the trickling blossoms
> by the ancient stone.
>
>   (*Ana*, 192)

Argos, who recognises Ulysses in what is perhaps the most memorable moment of the whole *Odyssey* (Book XVII, 291-2) here 'recognises' Christ as the fulfilment of the ideas of saviour and hero that Ulysses has represented. It is, in David Jones, a 'recognition scene' carried off with great power and panache; it is a moment in which many of the energies stored up by *The Anathemata* achieve a sudden and vivid release.

Both the tendency toward the 'creation of myth' and the 'Celticity' of Jones's imagination are apparent also in the two dramatised scenes in 'Mabinog's Liturgy' in which the liturgy of Christ's birth is celebrated. The first is a vision of Gwenhwyfar (the Welsh Guinevere), wife of Arthur, leaning to the stone of a Christmas mass; the second a conversation between the 'malkins three', the Welsh witches Marged, Mal Fay and Mabli. Both episodes celebrate the Christmas story and particularly the role of Mary in that story. Gwenhwyfar is both woman and symbol, described, Hermione-like, as 'the breathing marble' and 'the proud column', so that when she bows to the altar stone, it is as stone leaning to stone, the native insular tradition held static in a ritual gesture:

> So, wholly super-pellissed of British wild-woods, the chryselephantine column (native the warm blood in the blue veins that vein the hidden marbles, the lifted abacus of native gold) leaned, and toward the Stone.
>
>   (*Ana*, 203)

In her radiant beauty, Gwenhwyfar is a type of Mary; but the Marian theme is carried more centrally by the dialogue of the three witches around the idea 'No great thing but what there's a woman behind it, sisters.' (*Ana*,

214) These are very learned witches whose conversation at one point embraces a collocation of Virgil's fourth ('messianic') eclogue and the biblical accounts of Christ's nativity; and the climax of their discourse presents the Incarnation as a loving co-operation between the divine and the human will.

The apocalyptic strain evident in some of the conversation of the witches is explicit in the section of 'Mabinog's Liturgy' lying between the Gwenhwyfar scene and the witches scene, the Boast of Christ. Like the climactic Boast of Dai Greatcoat in *In Parenthesis*, this is modelled on the Celtic and Anglo-Saxon vaunting convention (Jones has in mind particularly the boast of Taliessin at the court of Maelgwyn); and it presents Christ as Celtic cult-hero and fulfilment of Egyptian, Greek and Roman deities. Then the end of 'Mabinog's Liturgy' turns to emphasise the continued liturgical presence of this cult-hero in human history by evoking the three masses of Christmas said in the Roman churches of St. Mary Major and St. Anastasia. And in this, perhaps the most sacramental, part of *The Anathemata*, the liturgy of this 'mabinog' is sung not only by poet and priest, but by nature itself:

>   Of Liber
>   perhaps from over the Sleeve
>   made confluent with the lucid gift
>   our naiads never fail to bring
>   parthenogenic from the rock
>   quick by high valleys, or
>   meandering slow and
>   by the wide, loamed ways, by sallowed way
>   sign the whole anatomy of Britain
>   with his valid sign
>   (out to where the nereids
>   bring in the shoal-gift: also Him, in sign).
>   (*Ana*, 204)

VIII   Sherthursdaye and Venus Day

The final section of *The Anathemata* completes the poem in the fullest sense of the word—fulfils it, and closes its circle. The title evokes Maundy Thursday ('Sherthursdaye' in Malory) and Good Friday ('and they call Good Friday Dydd Gwener y Groglith, Venus Day of the Lesson of the Cross', we are told in the preface to *Epoch and Artist*[31]) which together represent for David Jones the centre of the eucharistic mystery in the Christian liturgy—a significance confirmed and strengthened, as we have already seen, by his reading of Maurice de la Taille. The action performed in the 'lighted apses' of the Thursday is, for David Jones, indissolubly linked to the death on the 'spoil-dump' of the Friday. 'Sherthursdaye and Venus Day' is, then, a meditation on the joint significance of Christ's crucifixion and the institution of the eucharist. The mass, in its action of anamnesis, *'makes sense* of everything' for Jones;[32] and in this concluding section of his poem, the eucharistic act is viewed as the fulfilment of those processes of preparation celebrated throughout *The Anathemata*—'Here, to the Genius of this *familia* of new-*gens* founders inaugurally met./Informed from before history proper:/from the boundary time'. (*Ana*, 229)

In the action performed in the supper-room and on the hill, Christ is viewed as the fulfilment of all the poem's mythic heroes. He is 'like the hidden lords in the West-tumuli' who appear in the hill-parenthesis of 'Rite and Fore-time'; he is the hero who, like Peredur, 'frees the waters' and 'asks the question'; he is John Barleycorn who 'must be broken off at knee'; he is a Roman *paterfamilias* sacrificing for the benefit of his family; he is, in the terms of Biblical typology, Melchisedek, 'the stirpless lord'; he is Triptolemus; he is, in short, 'the *signum*'. In such 'fulfilments', Christ is evoked in majestic, sacred, prophetic and apocalyptic guise, the splendid, vested hero of medieval iconography. But 'Sherthursdaye and Venus Day' also portrays the pathetic Christ: the hill of Calvary, the last of the poem's hill-sites, reduces the creator of vast cosmic plenty to weeping and thirsting from a 'spoil-dump':

>   His cry
> from the axile stipe
>   at the dry node-height
> when the dark cloud brights the trembling lime-rock.
> (All known clouds distil showers.
> Is there no water in that dark cloud
>   for the parched lime-face?
> What unknown cloud then, is this?)
>
> As the bleat of the spent stag
>   toward the river-course
> he, the *fons*-head
>   pleading, *ad fontes*
> his desiderate cry:
>   SITIO.

(*Ana*, 237)

Christ is present, then, in the final section of *The Anathemata*, in all of the forms in which he has been understood by Christian tradition: as the fulfilment of myth and history (the 'Pantocrator'), and as the broken human scapegoat.

The whole of *The Anathemata* reaches its climax and conclusion in a presentation of the crucifixion which situates it in the terrifying context of the true nature, or 'kind', of the world in which it occurs. The 'dreaming arbor' is placed at the centre of a scene in which birds of prey screech their 'cawed madrigals' and search for their 'kindly food'. The final questions prompted here—'Who furthers the lammergyer? Who prevents the straight crow-flight? Who goes before the doings of such kind of fowl?' (*Ana*, 240)—, questions about the nature of justice and mercy which inevitably summon Tennyson's *In Memoriam* to mind, are 'answered' when the death evoked here is seen also as a marriage. Christ is imagined, in a reference to a marriage-god discovered in Augustine's *City of God*, as 'this Jugatinus of the noose, yoked for his nuptials on Skull Ridge'. (*Ana*, 241) Towards the very end of the poem the image recurs in a passage which is, in fact, a wedding celebration:

> But the fate of death?
> Well, that fits The Gest:
> How else be coupled of this Wanderer
> whose viatic bread shows forth a life?
> —in his well-built *megaron*.
> If not by this Viander's own death's monument
> by what bride-ale else lives his undying Margaron?
> —whose only threnody is Jugatine
> and of the *thalamus:* reeds then! and minstrelsy.
> (Nor bid Anubis haste, but rather stay:
> for he was whelped but to discern a lord's body).
>
> (*Ana*, 243)

Jones would have known Leon Bloy's description of the mass as 'an agony of holocaust accompanied by nuptial songs';[33] and the end of *The Anathemata*, whose 'only threnody is Jugatine', whose only death-lament is an epithalamion, is, in tone and meaning, a combination of those energies and impulses and convictions which sustain the final paradoxical assertion of Eliot's *Little Gidding*, that

> All manner of thing shall be well
> When the tongues of flame are in-folded
> Into the crowned knot of fire
> And the fire and the rose are one

and Auden's resolving image at the end of 'Compline', as he tries to 'propitiate/what happens from noon till three', in his prayer

> That we, too, may come to the picnic
> With nothing to hide, join the dance

> As it moves in perichoresis,
> > Turns about the abiding tree.

The end of *The Anathemata* has something of Eliot's magisterial calm, something of Auden's childlike trust.

But in Jones the final affirmation must still contend with that anguished sense of cultural breakdown which is emphasised again at the end of 'Sherthursdaye and Venus Day' as it had been at the beginning of 'Rite and Fore-Time'. From the poem's opening page, in which the rite is enacted 'at the sagging end and chapter's close', the whole of *The Anathemata* has fallen under the shadow of an awareness that 'dead symbols litter to the base of the cult-stone, that the stem by the palled stone is thirsty, that the stream is very low'. (*Ana*, 50) Now that the poem has brought before us all these 'symbols' once again, and that 'the stem by the palled stone' has been viewed in its original forms as 'the axile stipe', the question which the whole of *The Anathemata* poses about its cultural and religious inheritance is posed again in its most intense, gnomic form:

> Failing
> > (finished?) West
> your food, once.
>
> > > > (*Ana*, 231)

The question is insistently present throughout the poem; and it is significant that the final lines of *The Anathemata*, which suggest and summon a sense of continuity and coherence, a belief in transformation and fulfilment, do so not only in statement but in yet another interrogative:

> He does what is done in many places
> what he does other
> > he does after the mode
> of what has always been done.
> What did he do other
> > recumbent at the garnished supper?
> What did he do yet other
> > riding the Axile Tree?
>
> > > > (*Ana*, 243)

Notes

1. *Lives of the Poets: A Selection* (London, 1975), p. 264.
2. *The Colours of Clarity*, op. cit., p. 122.
3. *IP*, p. x.
4. *EA*, p. 29. The phrase is quoted from Ifor Williams who cites it as the way the Welsh bards referred to themselves.
5. *David Jones, Artist and Writer* (Manchester, 1971), p. 119.

6. *David Jones: An Exploratory Study* (London, 1975), p. 50.
7. *Welsh Poems: Sixth Century to 1600* (London, 1973), p. 11. This introduction first appeared in *The Burning Tree* (London, 1957).
8. Blamires, op. cit., p. 118.
9. *Norton Anthology*, op. cit., pp. 559-60.
10. '*The Anathemata* de David Jones, Poème Epique et Eucharistique', *Etudes Anglaises*, Juillet-Sept 1971, 241.
11. *Commentary*, p. 83. Hague's analogy is made with specific reference to 'Rite and Fore-Time'.
12. 'Anathemata', *Blackfriars*, xxiv, no. 403, 455.
13. 'The Present Past in *The Anathemata* and Roman Poems' in Roland Mathias (ed.), *David Jones: Eight Essays on His Work as Writer and Artist* (Llandysul, 1976), p. 53.
14. René Hague, *Commentary*, p. 113, insists that there are two separate voyages described in this section, the first ending in Phaleron, and only the second arriving in 'Lear-sea'. He cites a private letter from Jones which indicates that this is, indeed, intended to be the case. But the typography of the poem as we have it fails to provide for such a reading; and, as Jones himself says in his letter that 'the matter is of no great consequence', it seems best to read 'Middle-Sea and Lear-Sea', as all ordinary readers inevitably will, as if only one voyage is involved.
15. 'Trystan ac Essyllt by David Jones', *Agenda*, 11 no. 4-12 no. 1, Autumn-Winter 1973-4, 50-53. Jones was particularly familiar with the work of EGR Taylor, and a book she published after *The Anathemata*, *The Haven-Finding Art* (London, 1956), is very useful for a deeper understanding of the poem. David Jones's library contains numerous books on the sea and on seafaring.
16. 'Some Recent Paintings by David Jones', *Agenda*, 5 nos. 1-3, Spring-Summer 1967, 100. Clark does not name the painting he is describing, but he must mean either *Tangled Cup* of 1949 or *Flowers in a Chalice* of 1954.
17. The text of the first and subsequent editions prints a full stop after 'again'. This seems to me quite clearly wrong, as I have argued in 'Textual Problems in *The Anathemata*', *David Jones Society Newsletter*, no. 9, October 1977, p. 2. There are still many errors in the present edition of the poem, including a number known to have been marked for correction by David Jones himself.
18. See Colin Wilcockson (ed.), *David Jones: Letters to William Hayward* (London, 1979), facing p. 40.
19. A letter from Jones cited in Chute, 'Anathemata', op. cit., p. 459.
20. 'In Illo Tempore', *Gaul*, p. 22.
21. *IP*, p. 84.
22. *The Colours of Clarity*, p. 125.
23. I am indebted for this suggestion to Nicolas Jacobs.
24. Noon, *Poetry and Prayer*, op. cit., p. 343.
25. *EA*, p. 194.
26. Allan Wade (ed.), *The Letters of W. B. Yeats* (London, 1954), p. 922.
27. *Finnegans Wake* (London, 1939; 1964 edn.), p. 213.
28. *EA*, p. 85.
29. *IP*, p. 183.
30. *EA*, p. 39.
31. ibid., p. 18.
32. Letter to Lewis, p. 20, where he is actually quoting Lewis himself.
33. It is cited in D'Arcy, *The Mass and the Redemption*, op. cit., p. 79.

CHAPTER IV

Making This Thing Other: The 'Form' of the Poem

We already and first of all discern him making this thing other. His groping syntax, if we attend, already shapes . . .

(*Ana*, 49)

'Every great imaginative conception is a vortex into which everything under the sun may be swept. "All other men's worlds," wrote Coleridge once, "are the poet's chaos." ' Thus Livingstone Lowes at the end of *The Road to Xanadu*, a work which has been considered influential on David Jones.[1] Certainly the 'content' of *The Anathemata* is likely to evoke for the reader the sort of Joycean cry David Jones allows himself when confronting the compendiousness of Joyce's own work—'My colonial, wardha bagful!'[2] Sitting on the page on top of its long stilts of notes, *The Anathemata* proclaims itself immensely learned, allusive, encyclopaedic, and looks, indeed, like the work of a man determined to write both an *Ancient Mariner* itself *and* Lowes's immense gloss on it. The diversity of Jones's material has prompted comparison with *Finnegans Wake*, that other work of notorious unclassifiability; and the enormous complexity of its structure, seen as labyrinthine, as digressive and parenthetical, has provoked comparison with a favourite work of Jones's, Langland's *Piers Plowman*.[3]

In David Jones's prose writings, all sorts of convolution and complexity of design are celebrated in themselves, whether in the poetry of Hopkins, of Smart and of Langland, or in the prose of Joyce, in the arts of the La Tène culture—'the intricate arabesques of Kells, the involved and exacting patterns of Welsh bardic versification'[4]—or in the art of the native English genius in the Opus Anglicanum, in Nicholas Hilliard. In his essay, 'An Aspect of the Art of England',[5] such patterned intricacies are actually seen as the sign of an indigenously 'British' art, evoking a sense of the island as 'Pretanic', the name that Diodorus Siculus derived from the Priten or Picti, whose tribal name is etymologically connected with words actually *meaning* 'speckled' or 'mottled'. 'Not only is our land a most mottled, dappled, pied, partied and brindled land,' writes Jones in this essay, alluding to Hopkins's 'Pied Beauty', 'but so is our character, and so is the physical structure beneath . . . so also in a curious way is our art'.[6] There is no doubt that the natural push of David Jones's imagination is towards such mottled intricacy, and that the forms he finds—for the mind, he tells us in the preface to *The Anathemata*, is a 'hunter of forms', '*venator formarum*'—will themselves be intricate, complex and 'brindled'. Such forms seem to him, by lifting up what he calls 'a flowery, starry, intertwined image',[7] peculiarly reflective of his own composite inheritance. They work also towards that knotted intensity of utterance which is, for Jones, the essential mark of the well-made: all art, he once said in an interview, should be dedicated to 'making significant as much as possible in as compact a space as possible'.[8] *The Anathemata* should be regarded as a self-conscious continuation of, and contribution to, this native British formal tradition by a poet acutely conscious of its permanent relevance and value.

But the complexity and elaboration of the poem, its formal 'difficulty', is also the result of Jones's sense—made explicit in the preface—of what he calls the 'requisite now-ness' (*Ana*, 15) of all true art. The point is made insistently in 'The Arthurian Legend' when Jones fails to discover such a quality in the work of Charles Williams. His complaint is that 'somewhere, between content and form, concept and image, sign and what is signified, a sense of the contemporary escapes.' 'What the artist lifts up,' he insists, 'must have a kind of transubstantiated actual-ness. Our images, not only our ideas, must be valid *now*.'[9] This is, we may take it, Jones's relatively muted statement of the same quality of feeling that informs Pound's more dramatic injunction in Canto LIII and in his essays, to 'make it new'. Jones is nowhere more thoroughgoing a modernist than in his rigorous insistence on the necessity of formal and structural experimentation. The possibilities for literary renewal opened up by the study of anthropology, in particular, were deeply enriching and suggestive to Jones, as they were to others of his generation. Indeed, when Eliot greeted *Ulysses* in a famous review in 1923 as a triumph of original form and christened this form the 'mythical method', deciding that 'Mr. Joyce is pursuing a method that others must pursue after him',[10] he could well have been defining a programme that David Jones has taken to an ultimate conclusion in the vast synthesis of mythologies that *The Anathemata* represents.

Yet Jones's poem, although it has grown, inevitably, as he acknowledges, out of the same sorts of preoccupation as the work of Joyce, Eliot and Pound, and has responded to the same possibilities of abandoning narrative structure in favour of mythical synthesis, is in no sense merely a later rehearsal of familiar themes and techniques, as J. C. F. Littlewood would have us believe when he labels the work 'a new (Roman Catholic) *Waste Land* by a new (London-Welsh) T. S. Eliot.'[11] *The Anathemata* has more recently been recognised by George Steiner as so different a thing from *The Waste Land* that it is possible for him to consider it a 'radical act, new and contemporaneous with Blake': 'suggestive of other potential orderings', it is to be thought 'among prolegomena to future forms'.[12] It is on this level of formal inventiveness that the poem should still disturb and excite us. Whatever Jones's sense of the difficulties inherent in the making of a long poem in his time, he commits himself fully to the 'tradition of the new', when, in his preface, he notes that the poet's problems can provoke 'a most unsuspected inventiveness'. (*Ana,* 23) Assimilating, and developing from, a range of formal models embracing both the medieval intricacies of Langland and the post-symbolist obliquenesses of *The Waste Land,* David Jones creates, in *The Anathemata,* an altogether new and entirely individual sort of poem. I want now to consider the formal principles at work in it, in an attempt to define the essential character of this 'radical act'.

As I pointed out at the beginning of the last chapter, the most intelligent attempts to define the form of *The Anathemata*—including David Jones's own, in his preface—all suggest some sort of unity-within-diversity. It is possible, I hope, at this stage in my argument, to generalise from my account of the poem's 'content' in that chapter by claiming that the essential theme in the work, the theme that gives unity and coherence to all the others in the poem, is, precisely, the theme of an underlying unity, or continuity, to be discovered, or 'uncovered', in the apparent discontinuity of our present cultural situation. The theme is given its most aphoristic expression in 'Middle-Sea and Lear-Sea':

> The adaptations, the fusions
> the transmogrifications
>   but always
> the inward continuities
>   of the site
>   of place.
>
>   (*Ana,* 90)

Adaptations, fusions, transmogrifications—of the landface and seaface in 'Rite and Fore-Time', of the central symbols of water, stone and wood throughout the poem, of our legends and myths and stories of origin, of religious belief and ritual and art, of language itself—together with the search for an essential continuity, a familiar and recurring 'shape', within these fusions: such things supply the content of *The Anathemata.*

David Jones's more customary word for these processes is 'metamorphosis'. He uses the word in a wide variety of contexts in his work, but always with the force and power of defining a complex of deeply held and achieved convictions, associations and attitudes; it is, indeed, as he says the word 'anamnesis' is, a 'key-word' in his 'deposits'. In taking issue with what he sees as Bernard Berenson's narrow-minded Hellenism, for instance, he insists that 'it is only the *numina* of localities and differentiated traditions that could have dictated the metamorphoses in any and every art.' In the work of George Borrow he discovers a 'continuity' with the Wales of the past, 'in spite of the enormous cultural metamorphosis.' 'Strange are the metamorphoses' in the legend of Arthur. And, in the major essay, 'Art and Sacrament', he observes of our present situation that 'no metamorphosis since pre-historic times is in any way comparable to the metamorphosis that we are now undergoing.'[13] In *The Anathemata*, the word is given its geological signification when the 'New Light' is discovered beaming 'through all metamorphs or whatever the pseudomorphoses' (*Ana*, 74); and the processes of pre-history are embraced by the word made adjectival in one of the poem's many theatrical images:

>   There's where the world's a stage
>   for transformed scenes
>   with metamorphosed properties
>   for each shifted set.
>
> (*Ana*, 62)

The process of metamorphosis is seen, in short, as the essential mode of life on earth, and as the means by which our arts, our religions, our cultures, come into being. We realise ourselves by 'making this thing other' in the process of artefacture commemorated at the beginning of the poem. The thematic centre and heart of *The Anathemata* is to be found in the various processes of metamorphosis which it both celebrates and enacts: the poem's preoccupation with unity-within-diversity is the result of Jones's belief that 'There is only one tale to tell even though the telling is patient of endless development and ingenuity and can take on a million variant forms.' (*Ana*, 35)

In his essays, Jones is frequently concerned with problems of the relation between 'form' and 'content' in a work of art. His richest satisfactions come when he finds a deep unity, or wedding, of the two, as he does in early Welsh poetry. He discovers there 'a very compressed sort of poetry' in which 'the form and the content, the sound and the meaning, are inextricably one.' He compares such poetry to the visual art of other Celtic countries in which 'questions of the formal and the contential hardly arise because what we see is the visual image of their union.' And it is in the work of Joyce that he finds the most perfect modern example of this compression and unity: 'it was just this total oneness of form and content', he tells us, 'that the unflinching integrity of Joyce was determined to achieve in literary form; it was not for nothing that he looked steadfastly at a page from Kells.' Elsewhere, Joyce is referred to, very revealingly, as 'a master of the metamorphic who, in one medium alone, commands the incantational power of a number of media.'[14]

In *The Anathemata*, David Jones is perhaps visually signalling an intention to attempt a similar unity of form and content by publishing, as the first of his illustrations to the work (after the dedication), his inscription of a phrase from 'Anna Livia Plurabelle', 'Northmen's thing made southfolk's place', which he uses in one of his essays, 'The Arthurian Legend', to demonstrate how 'concept and universality are married to the local and the particular.'[15] What he calls in this essay the 'secret marriage'—of the universal and the particular, of content and form—is, I think, attempted by David Jones himself in *The Anathemata* in his arrangement of the pre-existent fragments of his writing in consonance with the central theme, or 'content', of the work: *The Anathemata* will be seen to have an integrated unity and coherence if we grant it what I would like to call 'metamorphic form', David Jones's unique contribution to the formal possibilities of the modern long poem.

The concept is one that Jones comes very close to defining himself in relation both to Celtic tradition and to the poem that is a constant focus of his attention, Coleridge's *Rime of the Ancient Mariner*.[16] Of the former, he observes in 'The Myth of Arthur' that 'The folk tradition of the insular Celts seems to present to the mind a half-aquatic world . . . it introduces a feeling of transparency and interpenetration of one element with another, of transposition and metamorphosis.'[17] And of Coleridge's poem he writes, in a way that even more obviously suggests the procedures of *The Anathemata*, that the poem's 'allusions are themselves elusively presented, for its imagery has a metamorphic quality. With swift artistry, with something akin to the conjurer's sleight of hand, the images seem now this, now that, a little like the shape-shifting figures in Celtic mythology.'[18] Before considering the metamorphic quality which I believe to inhere in the poem's major form, I wish firstly, taking this cue from David Jones himself, to examine, briefly, the more local metamorphic qualities of its imagery.

The sense of history in *The Anathemata*, in its diversities and continuities, is mediated largely through a contemplation of the artefacts which various cultures and civilisations have left behind, and which now embody their intrinsic meaning and quality. The sense of continuity in a tradition of 'making' is conveyed often by linguistic and imagistic transformations, or metamorphoses; artefacts from widely separated periods and cultures are related, within the generous harmonic reconciliation of the poem, in linked verbal descriptions. The Willendorf 'Venus', the Greek *kouroi*, and post-medieval art are established in fundamental human connection when, of the Willendorf statue, Jones wonders 'whose man-hands god-handled the Willendorf stone' (*Ana*, 59); of the *kouroi*, he discovers that 'man-limb stirs in the god-stones' (*Ana*, 91); and, in later art-work, 'The god still is balanced/in the man-stones' (*Ana*, 94). The central image for the creation of art, an infusion of 'god' into the work of 'man' (a concept, one may think, Lawrentian in its rich suggestiveness), is, in each case, transmitted through a subtly varied linguistic formula, so that the inner nature of the particular work is evoked at the same time as its connection with others in a continuity of creation is established.

Similarly, the Venus and its maker are brought into relation with the Celts of 185 BC and their 'scratched memorial' (*Ana*, 184) and with one of the inhabitants of 'Angle-Land', through another verbal metamorphosis. Of the Venus-maker, the poem asks,

> Who were his *gens*-men or had he no *Hausname* yet
> no *nomen* for his *fecit*-mark
>   the Master of the Venus?
>
> (*Ana*, 59)

Of the buried remains of the Anglo-Saxon, the question is:

> What was his *Hausname*?
>   he whose North Holstein urn
> they sealed against the seep of the Yare?
>
> (*Ana*, 113)

And, of the Celts—now, in 185 BC, being embraced by the Greek *imperium*—we are told that they are

> By their *Hausnamen* no longer called, their *nomina*
> already Anatolian:
> not now of *Wald* or *llan*
>   but, of the *polis*.
>
> (*Ana*, 185)

Again, the verbal forms in which all are presented dramatise their essential nature: the identity of the Venus Master is lost in the recessions of prehistory; the Anglo-Saxon is 'defined' by his Germanic funerary urn and his burial site by a Norfolk river; the Celts are situated at the point when the unsubdued intractability of their local culture has been subsumed under the civilised order of the Greek city-state. But the forms, metamorphosing around the word '*Hausname*', imply the continuity of 'shape' to be discerned below the surface distinctions of these widely separated cultures: all are embraced within the '*Hausname*' of the human family. The discernment of such a shape might be said, indeed, to be the true origin and end of *The Anathemata*: 'We already and first of all discern him making this thing other' at the beginning of the poem, and the moments at which the shapes of our cultures are imposed, and at which they metamorphose, are the moments which the poem attempts to 'discern' for us.

This local verbal metamorphosis, in which different occasions of history are brought into relation, is one of the poem's constant and characteristic procedures: it knits, or 'interweaves', Jones's huge coat of many colours in various intricate details of its design. London's churches are related in this way to the temples of Troy when London is described as 'Lud's town of megara' (*Ana,* 165) while Troy is 'the laughless Megaron' (*Ana,* 56); and both receive a metamorphic fulfilment on the poem's final page where the Church itself is 'his well-built *megaron*' (*Ana,* 243). The word 'laughless', used of Troy, is picked up again to describe the goddess-whore dreamt of by the shipman's boy in 'Middle-Sea and Lear-Sea', 'laughless little Telphousa' (*Ana,* 102), and is given resonance and depth by its association with 'Agelastos Petra' (the 'laughless rock'), the cult-object of pre-Hellenic Eleusis cited in 'Rite and Fore-Time' and referred to again in the text of 'Middle-Sea and Lear-Sea'. In a similar way, the helmsman of 'Keel, Ram, Stauros' with his 'stanced feet' (*Ana,* 181) is a metamorphosis of the *kouroi* of 'Middle-Sea and Lear-Sea', 'stanced solemn' (*Ana,* 91). There are larger patterns of repetition in the poem, associated with stone, water, wood and mountains, which work in a similarly insistent way; and I want to complete this discussion of the poem's local metamorphic quality by considering the representative images of mountains and hills as they echo through the work with, often, an extremely rich and original range of metamorphic implication.

This image-train is put in motion in the poem, almost subliminally, when the opening is set 'within the railed tumulus' (*Ana,* 51), an image which views the Christian altar, built over the relics of a saint, as a fulfilment of pre-Christian burial places under mounds or 'tumuli'. But the richest significance of the image, for David Jones, arises from the fact that Christ died on a hill; and Calvary is particularised first before the long hill parenthesis in 'Rite and Fore-Time' and again, much more fully, as the 'spoil-dump' of 'Sherthursdaye and Venus Day'.[19] Between these two points, which set the significance of the image, it undergoes a remarkable variety of metamorphoses and transformations which connect it with many of the most important themes in the poem.

The parenthetical passage of 'Rite and Fore-Time' (*Ana,* 55-8) echoes to the words 'under' and 'down' which become, in *The Anathemata* as a whole, both literal geological sitings and metaphorical terms for the cultural 'deposits' (itself, of course, a geological metaphor) lying 'under' us. They lie 'under' us also in the sense that they sustain us in being; and mountains are celebrated in this passage for their human significance as 'help-heights' and, in the associated image of the cavern, as 'efficacious asylums'. (*Ana*, 55) 'What's under works up,' as the Lady of the Pool insists, and this central fact of geology, of archaeology, of culture, and of the individual human psyche, is carried particularly, here and then subsequently throughout the poem, by what *In Parenthesis* calls 'the persistent Celtic theme of armed sleepers under the mounds',[20] the idea of the hero lying below the land who will stir again to aid his people in time of confusion. It is by making Christ himself part of this tradition that David Jones brings to a brilliant and extraordinary conclusion the metamorphoses of his mountain imagery.

The process is inaugurated when he draws an analogy between hills and the very protruberant breasts of the Willendorf Venus, representative of the *genetrix* without which no life, human or artistic, would be possible:

> How else we?
> or he, himself?
> whose name is called He-with-us
> because he did not abhor the uterus.
> Whereby these uberal forms
> are to us most dear
> and of all hills
> the most august.
>
> (*Ana*, 75)

Having established this connection, Jones can then, much later in the poem, imagine Christ as a mound-dweller in the 'tumulus' of his mother's womb (the image works through a kind of 'metaphysical' fusion):

> Marquis of demarking waters
> Warden of the Four Lands
> from her salined deeps
> from the cavern'd waters
> (where she ark'd him) come.
> His members in-folded
> like the hidden lords in the West-tumuli
> for the nine dark calends gone.
>
> (*Ana*, 224-5)

Given this accumulated context of association, the climax of *The Anathemata* achieves a deep and terrible ironic force. Here, Christ cries from 'the dry node-height/when the dark cloud brights the trembling lime-rock' (*Ana*, 237), and the poem's hill imagery undergoes its final metamorphosis into a particular evocation of Calvary. Christ, the sleeping lord of his mother's womb, has stirred to life only, apparently, to be put savagely to death. The metamorphoses of this image have also urged what I take it to be the whole point of the poem to insist: the process by which the divine penetrates the human is made to seem natural, inevitable and, as it were, a casual fact of human observation. The poem's religious meaning is incorporated into the experience of geology, of artefacture, of human generation. Again, *The Anathemata*, in its smallest details, is a radically incarnational poem.

Formally, then, the elaboration, paralleling, metamorphosing of his image-patterns is David Jones's means of binding together his huge poem in its local detail; and these patterns also enact an exact formal correspondence to his central theme of continuity-within-diversity. The poem's imagery is a kind of 'work of transaccidentation', like the Lady of the Pool's mist, and might well be thought of in the way the Lady thinks of her source material:

> Though there's a deal of subsidence hereabouts even so:
>   gravels, marls, alluviums
> here all's alluvial, cap'n, and as unstable as these old annals
> that do gravel us all.
>
>   (*Ana,* 164)

But, if this is true of the poem's local imagery and language, it is all the more true, I believe, of the containing modes of its organisation, its principles of major form. Introducing the poem for a recording, David Jones observed that '*The Anathemata* is cyclic in character and however wide the circle, the action of the Mass is central to it and insofar as a circle can be said to have a "beginning" or an "end", it begins and ends with the Mass.'[21] *The Anathemata* is indeed 'circular' in that its end returns us to its beginning, and both end and beginning are *literally* set 'in the time of the mass', the opening of the poem introducing us to a contemporary priest sacrificing at the altar, and its close presenting us with Christ's own institution of the eucharistic sacrifice which lies at the centre of the meaning of the mass. It is sometimes thought, however,—and Jones's preface may be considered to sanction the idea—that the liturgy of the mass provides a structure for the poem in the sense that the whole of *The Anathemata* is somehow intended to take place in the consciousness of someone attending a mass. Jeremy Hooker, for instance, thinks it 'helpful, initially, to think of *The Anathemata* as the meditations of a man attending mass', although this does not, he thinks, confine the poem 'to a specific temporal or spatial dimension'.[22] But if the poem is not limited or confined in some way by this idea, then the idea itself seems not particularly 'helpful' and, indeed, unnecessarily complicating. It seems, in short, about as helpful—or as misleading— as the idea, inspired by Eliot himself in his notes, that *The Waste Land* somehow represents the 'consciousness' of Tiresias. Both Eliot's poem, and *The Anathemata*, are damaged if they are thought narrowly restricted to a single perceiving vision.

The real significance of the mass for Jones's poem is, I think, that this eucharistic celebration is, essentially, a 'making other'—of bread and wine into Christ's body and blood in the act of consecration, of the quotidian processes of human existence into the order of liturgical worship and ritual. The mass is, in fact, an ultimate metamorphic action, and it is as such that it provides a sustaining shape for *The Anathemata*. It is intimately related to all the ship voyages of the poem for, as we are told in an important note, 'What is pleaded in the Mass is precisely the argosy or voyage of the Redeemer, consisting of his entire sufferings and his death, his conquest of hades, his resurrection and his return in triumph to heaven. It is this that is offered to the Trinity . . . on behalf of us argonauts and of the whole argosy of mankind'. (*Ana*, 106)[23] The poem's voyage imagery, as I have indicated in the previous chapter, is in a constant process of metamorphosis and is often, in fact, intertwined with imagery drawn from the mass. The Maundy Thursday supper room in the opening section is being made 'ship-shape . . . all Bristol-fashion' for the 'Master of her' (*Ana*, 53), while the ship voyage of 'The Lady of the Pool' metamorphoses gradually into the imagery of eucharistic celebration:

> All her sheer
> the entire trembling keel-length of her vessel of burden
> silvered of
> driven rain
> gilted of
> bends of paly light
> white as the Housel of spume.
> The tilted heavers
> her oblation-stone
> immenser hovers dark-ápse her.
>
> (*Ana*, 140)

The two major containing image-patterns of the poem—the mass, the voyage—thus blend into each other, or 'metamorphose', at moments of greatest intensity in a way that mirrors, in the poem's major form, the local imagistic metamorphoses I have been considering in this chapter.

The significance of the mass as a constant source of imagery, and a constant focus of reference and allusion, is related to the strain of theatrical imagery in the poem, in which human life is seen as a brief drama enacted on the stage of cosmic history.[24] In 'Rite and Fore-Time', the emergence of man from earlier forms is evoked in this way:

> The mimes deploy:
>   anthropoid
>   anthropoi.
> Who knows at what precise phase, or from what floriate green-room, the Master of Harlequinade, himself not made, maker of sequence and permutation in all things made, called us from our co-laterals out, to dance the Funeral Games of the Great Mammalia, as, long, long, long before, these danced out the Dinosaur?
>
>   (*Ana*, 63)

And some of the processes described in this opening section of the poem are said to occur 'Just before they rigged the half-lit stage for dim-eyed Clio to step with some small confidence the measures of her brief and lachrymal pavan.' (*Ana*, 68) If human life itself is seen as drama, then the liturgy is, for David Jones, a great religious drama in which life is uttered and transformed, metamorphosed into the intense articulation of ritual. The point is made by Gregory Dix whose *The Shape of the Liturgy* was, as we have seen, profoundly influential on David Jones's thought:

> It is not strange that the eucharist should have this power of laying hold of human life, of grasping it not only in the abstract but in the particular concrete realities of it, of reaching to anything in it, great impersonal things that rock whole nations and little tender human things of one man's or one woman's living or dying— laying hold of them and translating them into something beyond time.[25]

This is the most apprehensible level on which it is possible to understand what Jones means when he says, quoting Saunders Lewis, that the mass '*makes sense* of everything'. Because the mass is, in itself, a transforming incorporation of so much of significance in human life, *The Anathemata* uses it as a model for its own transforming incorporations, safely gathering everything in.[26]

What the mass manages to 'gather in' in the poem is vast. It incorporates the dead of pre-history in 'Rite and Fore-Time', through the reiterated *dona eis requiem* refrain, and the use of the *Dies Irae* sequence, from the requiem mass. It provides an insight, by analogy, into what happened, artistically, at Lascaux, where the phrase used to describe the creative process—doing 'in an unbloody manner'

>   what is done, without
> far on the windy tundra
> at the kill
> that the kindred may have life
>
>   (*Ana*, 60)—

is a reworking of the Council of Trent's definition of the manner in which the mass re-enacts Christ's sacrifice on Calvary. It provides a humanising context in which to understand the processes of geological transformation, as when 'Cronos reads the rubric, *frangit per medium*, when he breaks his ice like morsels, for the therapy and fertility of the land-masses'. (*Ana*, 69) And particular masses constantly supply the poem with phrases, refrains, a context of traditional liturgical usage which gathers depth and momentum as the poem progresses, until the ending of 'Mabinog's Liturgy' is a dense tissue of interwoven liturgical allusion.

But it is also the case that the poem takes the mass for its subject matter at particular points. As we have seen, it opens and closes in specific liturgical evocation. It presents, in 'Mabinog's Liturgy', the set-piece description of Gwenhwyfar's attendance at a Christmas midnight mass, which includes Jones's conflation of the gospel of the first mass of Christmas with Virgil's 'prophetic' fourth eclogue. And 'Mabinog's Liturgy' concludes in an evocation of the saying of two further Christmas masses in the Roman churches of St. Anastasia's and St. Mary Major's. Appropriately, then, it is a note to this section of the poem that presents us with the major significance of the mass for *The Anathemata*, when Jones cites Dix's definition of anamnesis: each thing gathered in, incorporated, by the mass is recalled in such a transforming way that it becomes 'here and now operative by its effects' (*Ana*, 205), and Jones wishes an analogous intensity for the recallings that comprise his own work. In a discussion in 'The Myth of Arthur' of what Malory has done with the Arthurian material he handles, Jones says that in Malory, 'all is gathered in, baptized if need be, somehow incorporated.'[27] It could well be claimed that the recallings of his own poem are, in some sense, 'baptized' by their incorporation into the Christian liturgy. Innocent of interpretation in themselves, they become, in Jones's hands, 'anathemata'. The cult-objects and artefacts of all kinds—Venus of Willendorf, Lascaux paintings, Greek *kouroi*, Latin plainchant, Gwenhwyfar's vestments—make 'here and now operative' the essential meaning and feeling of the cultures that produced them. They incarnate, and metamorphose into an apprehensible form, the understanding of human life, and of human history, of the ages they represent. For David Jones, the Roman mass, in all its transforming metamorphoses, incarnates, and makes again operatively present, in an objective form, the final purpose of human life and the final meaning of human history. *The Anathemata*, as a result, both celebrates this religious art form and uses its nature as a great ritualistic drama of incorporation, as a model and principle of metamorphic form.

But it is possible, in describing this 'shape' that the poem assumes, seriously to over-emphasise its liturgical and ritualistic quality. In fact, for a work that has seemed to some of its critics to smell not only of the lamp but of the thurible too, *The Anathemata* is full of noise and life—nourished, as D. S. Carne-Ross has said, by 'a great diversity and hubbub of human doing'.[28] The poem is an immense chorus of human voices, shouting, singing, cajoling, crying, praying. These voices often directly speak the poem: Eb Bradshaw, the Lady of the Pool, the sea-captain and his crew, the 'heath-hags' of 'Mabinog's Liturgy' are all present to us in their immediately recognisable and distinct tones of voice. In this sense, it is certainly profitable to regard the poem, at least partly, as a succession of dramatic monologues; and Jones's insistence that it is to be *heard*, that we should speak it aloud, and in particular accents and intonations, has this primary significance. *The Anathemata* is an intensely dramatic poem, a poem for the speaking voice in action—a point reinforced by the successful BBC radio broadcast made of it by Douglas Cleverdon.[29]

But a vast number of other characters enters the poem more obliquely, sometimes to glance out at us for only a line or two, and these figures share that metamorphic quality of 'shape-shifting' which Jones finds in the figures of Celtic mythology. They are often themselves mythological figures—Arthur, Clio, Calypso, Hector, Lamia, Igraine, Lud, Manawydan, but the list insists itself endlessly[30]—whom we watch merging, dissolving, renewing. These metamorphoses of the poem's *dramatis personae* involve us in a recognition of those fundamental patterns of human existence, the basic 'shapes' that human life and art have taken, with which Jones is preoccupied. Hugh Kenner has discovered in Joyce's work a principle of revealing the same shape in a variety of different stories which he calls 'homeomorphism'; and in Pound's *Cantos* a similar principle of the discovery of continuities is found to operate through a system of 'subject rhymes'. 'For the gods', writes Kenner, 'persist . . . Christ is Tammuz again; the personnel change, the names of the gods mutate, but the cults have analogous impulses, stubbornly conserving.'[31] *The Anathemata* moves through an encyclopaedic consideration of the personnel of our corporate mythologies into a very precise sense of this stubborn conservation.

Just as the technique of presenting material through insistent questioning works to create shimmering perspectives of alternative possibility in the poem, the constant transformations of its personnel create a sense of fluid dissolution between the boundaries of different myths, Homeric, Virgilian, Egyptian, Norse, Arthurian, Celtic, Christian. In this, Jones is certainly a true inheritor of the spirit of Frazer, who actually concludes *The Golden*

Bough with a purple passage on the continuities of pagan and Christian tradition:

> But Nemi's woods are still green, and as the sunset fades above them in the west, there comes to us, borne on the swell of the wind, the sound of the church bells of Rome ringing the Angelus.[32]

In his essay, 'The Myth of Arthur', David Jones considerably sophisticates Eliot's concept of the 'mythical method' and implies its all-embracing generosity in his own work:

> To conserve, to develop, to bring together, to make significant for the present what the past holds, without dilution or any deleting, but rather by understanding and transubstantiating the material, this is the function of genuine myth, neither pedantic nor popularizing, not indifferent to scholarship, nor antiquarian, but saying always: 'of these thou hast given me have I lost none.'[33]

It is significant that Jones here employs the term 'transubstantiating', drawn from eucharistic theology: his use of the metamorphoses of myth in *The Anathemata* is parallel to his use of the mass. Both work towards a totality of incorporation, a huge synthesis. And, as we saw earlier, it is possible to think of at least one section of the poem, 'The Lady of the Pool', as itself actually *creating* myth, as well as conserving and developing it.[34]

It is in this metamorphic synthesis of mythology that Jones extends, as a poetic technique, the structural principle, the 'mythical method', handled in varying ways by many of the important poets of the century. The synthesis that Jones constructs is one that creates, at its most intense, an extraordinary density and compaction of language. A passage from the end of Christ's Boast in 'Mabinog's Liturgy', if exceptional, may nevertheless be taken as indicative of this synthesis:

> Lar of Lares Consitivi
>   Himself the Lar and the garner
> broken under Marmor's sign.
>   But then, like Marmor *miles*
> that whets his weapon acute at both edges.
> Out from the mother (coronate of the daughter)
>   bearing the corn-stalks.
> Exact Archon (by whom Astráea on Themis)
>   Lord-Paraclete of the Assize—
> Yet who alone is named MISERICORS.
>
> (*Ana*, 209)

Christ is viewed here as fulfilling the myths of Greece and Rome. The 'shape' of Christ as warrior against sin and death, and as judge with the double-edged sword, is superimposed on the 'shape' of the Roman Mars, god of war. But Mars himself achieved this 'shape' from his original one as an agricultural deity; and, in this, Christ is also similarly 'shaped' through his connection with the wheat of the eucharist. But this connection suggests the further 'shapes' of the Roman *lares*, the household gods who were originally field deities (and hence 'consitivi', 'of sowing'), and of the Greek vegetation myth of Demeter and Persephone. The complex synthesis of the passage thus releases an understanding of an essential unity in human experience, through a demonstration of the very similar shapes in which human beings, throughout history, have focussed their understanding of themselves.

The passage I have just quoted is, of course, exceptional in its compaction of meaning and, thus, exceptional in its difficulty; but it is certainly the case that *The Anathemata* as a whole, in its own 'shape in words', writes this sort of understanding large. In the Christian fulfilment of myth, it therefore finds 'birthday and anniversary' (*Ana*, 51), and Christ and Mary, who might be regarded as the virtually anonymous hero and heroine of the final parts of the poem, act as implicit fulfilments of all the other male and female characters—of the ship-master and the Lady of the Pool; of the sleeping lords under their mounds and Athene Promachos; of Hector and Helen; of Arthur and Gwenhwyfar; of Triptolemus and Demeter. *The Anathemata* constitutes, indeed, a 'fusion of typic figures of great splendour and depth', a marriage of mythologies below the surface of their common shapes: it is, as Louis Bonnerot has remarked, 'un poème marial'.[35] And, in this, the poem enacts and dramatises for us that sense of identity that David Jones believes we should feel with all those behind us, or 'under' us, who have lived in order to create a sustaining culture. In this way, the mythical organisation of the poem also enforces an apprehension of its essential didactic point (I use the word deliberately, despite the fact that in the preface Jones disclaims 'any pretensions whatever of a didactic nature'). For it is precisely the crisis of *The Anathemata* that the sense of identity and continuity of tradition that it conveys to us is now under overwhelming threat, that the various metamorphoses of an abiding tradition are, 'at the sagging end and chapter's close' (*Ana*, 49), in danger of losing contact altogether with the familiar shapes in which we can recognise ourselves. For David Jones, our severance from them is a radical alienation. And this is exactly the point made by Jones's major formal innovation in the poem, an innovation which may also, I think, be regarded as a principle of 'metamorphic form', his annotation.

The word 'innovation' seems proper here, for although Jones is obviously profoundly aware of *The Waste Land* and its annotation, and had already comprehensively annotated *In Parenthesis*, *The Anathemata*, with its text deeply embedded in its notes, seems altogether a different matter. Although Jones asks us, '*when actually engaged upon the text*' (*Ana*, 43), to consult the notes only on points of pronunciation, virtually all readers, even after the most thorough acquaintance with the poem, will find this a practical impossibility. One's eye, and one's attention, are aware of the notes inevitably and necessarily while one reads the poem; they are an integral part of our experience of it. *The Waste Land*, we might say, is a poem with notes; *The Anathemata* is that different, new and disturbing thing, a poem-with-notes.

The notes to the poem are, as Jones makes explicit, symptomatic of the fissiparous state of the culture in which he is writing; they acknowledge the essential privacy of our individual traditions and keep open the lines of communication between author and readers by attempting to open up 'unshared backgrounds'.[36] The information they convey is genuinely informative: as Eliot himself said, perhaps with *The Waste Land* Possum-like in mind, '*The Anathemata* is unusual, in my experience of long poems with notes, in having notes which really do give useful information.'[37] They are much more akin, in their quirky individuality, to the notes Marianne Moore appends to her poems, than to Eliot's own farcical-solemn pieces of 'bogus scholarship'. Denise Levertov conveys their essential character when she urges that Jones is a poet 'in whom scholarship is an extension of intuitive knowledge':[38] the backgrounds sketched in, the relationships established, by the notes are themselves transformed by the immediacy of Jones's delighted and enthusiastic informativeness.

But part of the effect of the notes is to present the poem as a hugely elaborate riddle, as Auden pointed out in approval,[39] and to make some of our enjoyment of it the fascination of what Anthony Thwaite has called 'exalted code-cracking'.[40] Perhaps David Jones is right in thinking that this is the only way, now, that a poet with his largeness of concern and generosity of interest can proceed, and certainly the annotation does work towards a necessary understanding of matters that the poetry could not handle directly without its certain collapse into the flatulently reductive. Indeed it is possible to think of David Jones's combination of poem and notes as the severest and most thoroughgoing response imaginable to Eliot's belief, expressed in 'The Music of Poetry', that a modern long poem must contain varying intensities of prose and poetry and his insistence in *The Use of Poetry and the Use of Criticism* that 'for us, anything that can be said as well in prose can be said better in prose.'[41]

But I wonder if it is altogether too fanciful to see David Jones's poem-with-notes form in *The Anathemata* as yet a further, and ultimate, contribution to what I have characterised in this chapter as 'metamorphic form'.

Just as his densely allusive language, containing in the space of a few pages the combination of Greek, Latin, German, Welsh, English, is a constant, living reminder, in the very texture of the work, of the metamorphoses of our linguistic inheritance, a page of *The Anathemata* is, even typographically, an insistence on that process of transformation, metamorphosis, 'transubstantiation', 'making other', at the heart of the whole work. The words of the text are made to seem carefully chiselled, sculpted out of the surrounding stone of the notes. 'You must have a lumber room where you have habitation,' we are told in *In Parenthesis*;[42] and *The Anathemata* brings, as it were, the 'lumber-room' of the poet's word-hoard before us as insistently as the 'habitation' of his achieved poem. The 'poetry' of *The Anathemata* is deliberately not cast clear from the 'prose' of its origins; the word refined and perfected and chosen is caught in the clutter of its formation. We are confronted, on every page of the book, by David Jones himself 'making this thing other', transforming the raw material of his experience and reading into the form of his poetry: for, indeed, 'men can but proceed from what they know, nor is it for the mind of this flesh to practise poiesis, *ex nihilo.*' (*Ana*, 79)

It has been one of the central impulsions of modern poetry to create a large-scale structure, not dependent on narrative logic or continuity, but affecting the reader with that largeness of ambition, preoccupation and attention which the long poems of earlier centuries implicitly or explicitly claim. In *The Anathemata*, by extending the techniques available to him into a principle of what I have called here 'metamorphic form', David Jones has, I would claim, made a major contribution to the search for such structures. Complex, richly allusive, fascinatingly intricate, *The Anathemata* is nowhere more inclusively generous than in the wedding of possibilities—medieval, Celtic, Catholic, modernist—which its form achieves.

Notes

1. London, 1927; 1955 edn., p. 389. René Hague, in *David Jones*, op. cit., p. 43, claims that *The Road to Xanadu* suggested to Jones 'the *sort* of lines on which work could be done.'
2. *EA*, p. 18.
3. Nicolas Jacobs, 'The Sacramental Scene', *TLS*, 4 March 1977, p. 250. Whatever force there is in the analogy, one must doubt the usefulness of William Hayward's apparent attempt to relate the two poems through their mutual, self-conscious dependence on the four levels of allegory: see *Letters to William Hayward*, op. cit., especially Jones's courteous response to Hayward's comparison, 'well, it's a bit tidy' (p. 17).
4. *EA*, p. 198.
5. *Gaul*, pp. 59-62.

6. ibid., p. 59.
7. ibid.
8. Peter Orr (ed.), *The Poet Speaks* (London, 1966), p. 103.
9. *EA,* pp. 209, 210.
10. 'Ulysses, Order and Myth', 1923, reprinted in Ellmann and Feidelson (eds.), *The Modern Tradition* (New York, 1965), p. 681.
11. 'Joyce-Eliot-Tradition', op. cit., p. 337.
12. These phrases are taken from Steiner's remarks on Jones in *Extraterritorial* (London, 1972), p. 169, and *Language and Silence* (London, 1967; 1969 edn.), p. 342.
13. Cf. *EA,* pp. 270, 77, 213, 144.
14. ibid., pp. 57, 63, 64 and *Gaul,* p. 181.
15. *EA,* p. 210. The phrase from Joyce occurs in *Finnegans Wake,* p. 215.
16. The 'constancy' of Jones's fascination with the poem can be traced from his copper-engravings for an edition published by Douglas Cleverdon in Bristol in 1929; through the introduction to the poem which he wrote for a new edition of these engravings published by the Chilmark Press in 1964; up to the full version of this published separately by Cleverdon and Clover Hill Editions as *An Introduction to 'The Rime of the Ancient Mariner'* in 1972, and reprinted in *Gaul,* pp. 186-225. In his poetry, the *Rime* is alluded to in the opening part of *In Parenthesis,* 'The Many Men So Beautiful' (the next, unquoted line is, 'And they all dead did lie'), and was, he tells us, 'much in my mind during the writing of Part 3.' (See *IP,* p. 199) There are several allusions to the poem in the text of *The Anathemata;* and, in a note left in one of Jones's own copies of the poem, now in the National Library of Wales, he observes, of 'Keel, Ram, Stauros', that '*The Ancient Mariner* is behind a number of forms used in this section and elsewhere in *ANA. The Ancient Mariner* is one of the clues to *ANA?*'
17. *EA,* pp. 238-9.
18. *Gaul,* p. 190.
19. The significance of Calvary as a meeting-point between man and God is only one version of the ancient theme of mountains with this sort of implication. See Maud Bodkin, *Archetypal Patterns in Poetry* (London, 1934), where the image is traced in Virgil, Dante and Milton.
20. *IP,* p. 198.
21. See the notes to the record, *Readings from 'The Anathemata', 'In Parenthesis', 'The Hunt',* Argo PLP 1093.
22. *David Jones: An Exploratory Study,* op. cit., p. 32.
23. As I have, I hope, made clear in Chapter III, David Jones makes much use of the orthodox patristic tradition of the 'ship of the church' in his voyage imagery. But it is also interesting that Rees and Rees in *Celtic Heritage* (London, 1961), p. 314, observe that 'the theme of the otherworld voyage is one of the most distinctive in Celtic tradition.' On the patristic theme, see Jean Daniélou, *Primitive Christian Symbols* (London, 1964).
24. In using this metaphor, Jones was probably influenced by Collingwood and Myres, *Roman Britain and the English Settlements* (Oxford, 1936), where the opening chapter is entitled 'The Stage of History'.
25. p. 746.
26. See *EA,* p. 243: ' "All must be safely gathered in", as Mr. Stanley Spencer said to me with reference to the making of a picture (a more apt expression of the artist's business I never heard).'
27. *EA,* p. 250.
28. 'David Jones 1895-1974', *Arion,* NS, 1 no. 4, 1973-4, 705.

29. First broadcast on the BBC Third Programme, 5 May 1953. The broadcast includes an extraordinary performance by Dylan Thomas. Douglas Cleverdon, its producer, writes interestingly about it in 'David Jones and Broadcasting', *Poetry Wales*, 8 no. 3, Winter 1972, 72-81.
30. One of the fruits of research: there are, according to my mathematics, over two hundred proper names in the poem.
31. See *The Pound Era*, op. cit., pp. 34, 92, 368.
32. 1957 edn., p. 934.
33. *EA*, p. 243.
34. Recent critical writing about David Jones shows very interestingly how 'myth' can still be created and transmitted. William Blissett has suggested that Jones's use of the term 'Big Ship' in *In Parenthesis* to refer to the 'mythological, desired ship which would, at the termination of hostilities, bring all expeditionary men, maimed or whole, home again' (*IP*, p. 212) is, in fact, almost certainly Jones's own creation. See 'The Efficacious Word' in Roland Mathias (ed.), *David Jones: Eight Essays*, op. cit., p. 44. Blissett is very widely read indeed in the literature of the First World War and has found no other use of the term to confirm Jones's. But Paul Fussell, in his brilliant book, *The Great War and Modern Memory* (New York and London, 1975), p. 142, without actually citing Jones, refers to the 'Big Ship' as 'the troops' mythological, pseudo-Arthurian term'. Elsewhere in the book, Fussell shows himself deeply read in *In Parenthesis*, and one wonders if he is here transmitting the 'myth' which Jones has created. If he is, then Jones has here singlehandedly created, for readers of Fussell's book, what he calls in *In Parenthesis* a 'potent mythological theme'. (*IP*, p. 212)
35. '*The Anathemata* de David Jones', op. cit., 251.
36. See *Ana*, p. 14. The phrase is C. S. Lewis's in *Arthurian Torso* (London, 1948).
37. 'A Note on *In Parenthesis* and *The Anathemata*', op. cit., 22.
38. *The Poet in the World* (New York, 1973), p. 82.
39. 'A Contemporary Epic', *Encounter*, xii no. 2, February 1954, 67-71.
40. *Poetry Today, 1960-1973* (London, 1973), p. 9.
41. Cf. *On Poetry and Poets* (London, 1957), pp. 26-38 and *The Use of Poetry etc.* (London, 1933; 1964 edn.), p. 152.
42. *IP*, p. 90.

CHAPTER V

Returning to the Origin: The Achievement of the Poem

> What I call the 'auditory imagination' is the feeling for syllable and rhythm, penetrating far below the conscious levels of thought and feeling, invigorating every word; sinking to the most primitive and forgotten, returning to the origin and bringing something back, seeking the beginning and the end. It works through meanings, certainly, or not without meanings in the ordinary sense, and fuses the old and obliterated and the trite, the current, and the new and surprising, the most ancient and the most civilised mentality.
>
> T. S. Eliot, *The Use of Poetry and the Use of Criticism*

In an interview in 1964, David Jones discussed the quality of feeling he sensed in his generation during the earliest stages of the First World War. 'Everyone was joining up,' he says: 'We felt we were getting into history.'[1] The long essay, 'Art in Relation to War', makes it apparent how deeply this entry into history affected the young private soldier. As a result of his experience in the trenches, David Jones acquired a sense of identity with the common, anonymous foot-soldier throughout history. 'We can guess', he says, 'better than our immediate forebears, something of what a paid foot-soldier at Crécy *felt* about a damp bow-string and the heavy Picardy mud, and the relationship between these immediate, intimate, bodily-known things and the Plantaganet pretensions, the rising will of the French monarchy towards supremacy on French soil, and the credits of the Florentine banking houses.'[2] (There is perhaps no other single sentence in David Jones's prose writings that more succinctly witnesses to the combination in his work of empathetic imagination and historical scholarship.) The First World War took Private David Jones 'into history' in a way obviously unavailable to the non-combatants of his literary generation—a fact insisted on by Eliot in his 'Note of Introduction' to *In Parenthesis*. The war concentrated and focussed Jones's own sense of identity, for the regiment he joined in 1915—the London Welsh Battalion of the Royal Welch Fusiliers—brought him into direct, daily contact with, as it were, an incarnate objectification of the two strands of his own Anglo-Welsh heritage, his own personal 'history'. Of the men alongside whom he lived and fought, Jones writes, 'Nothing could be more representative. These came from

London. Those from Wales. Together they bore in their bodies the genuine tradition of the Island of Britain, from Bendigeid Vran to Jingle and Marie Lloyd. These were the children of Doll Tearsheet. Those are before Caractacus was.' In their speech Jones found 'a perpetual showing' of his own corporate inheritance; and to live with these men in those circumstances was to live with 'a consciousness of the past, the very remote, and the more immediate and trivial past; both superficially and more subtly.' The poem which he created out of this experience is a poem as much about the nature of this inheritance as it is about the conditions of war. *In Parenthesis* is a vivid record of the life of a true culture, in which to return to base is to 'know the homing perfume of wood burned, at the termination of ways; and sense here near habitation, a folk-life here, a people, a culture already developed, already venerable and rooted.' 'Getting into history' was, then, for David Jones, to experience at first-hand the creation, development and eventual extinction of this culture. In *In Parenthesis*, the stuff of cultural identity and coherence faces a very literal apocalyptic destruction:

> Nor time for halsing
> nor to clip green wounds
> nor weeping Maries bringing anointments
> neither any word spoken
> nor no decent nor appropriate sowing of this seed
> nor remembrance of the harvesting
> of the renascent cycle
> and return
> nor shaving of the head nor ritual incising for
> these *viriles* under each tree.
>   No one sings: Lully lully
> for the mate whose blood runs down.[3]

But if the First World War involved for David Jones the agonised personal witnessing of the destruction of a culture, it was also during this period that he began to sense the importance for him of the religion that was to supply the context for his life and work. 'It was I think sometime in 1917 somewhere in the neighbourhood of Ypres,' he tells us, 'that I first found myself wondering about the Catholic tradition. Four years later, in 1921, I found myself unable to do other than subscribe to that tradition.'[4] Jones describes this 'wondering' in a letter to René Hague in a way that, uniquely in the writings so far published, suggests the emotional compulsion behind his turning to the Catholic tradition. Coming unexpectedly on a celebration of mass in a remote out-house while scavenging for firewood, Jones is deeply impressed by the unity and solidarity manifested by the occasion: 'I felt immediately that oneness between the Offerand and those toughs that clustered round him in the dim-lit byre—a thing I had never felt remotely as a Protestant at the Office of Holy Communion in spite of the insistence in Protestant theology on "the priesthood of the laity".'[5] If all else in the history that David Jones had got himself into appeared to fall apart, there was here, uniquely it seemed, a centre that would hold.

The First World War, then, made David Jones the man and artist he was to become: it exposed him, in the most cruelly immediate way imaginable, to the realities of the historical process; it presented him with a living embodiment of the cultures of his own mixed tradition; it provided him with the experience at the heart of his first great poem; it forced on his attention the claims of the religion that was to become the accepted structure of belief in his life and the unifying 'system' of his work. It is not surprising that Jones constantly insists on the supreme importance that this war had in his own life: in his 'Autobiographical Talk', he tells us that 'the particular Waste Land that was the forward area of the West Front had a permanent effect upon me and has affected my work in all sorts of ways—so much so that it is impossible now for me to imagine myself without that period in the *ffosydd* in Gallia Belgica.'[6] And the overriding result of the experience was the irredeemable loss of former qualities of innocence: 'we have been forced to live history,' Jones writes, 'as Tennyson's generation was not.'[7]

If *In Parenthesis*—and, to a lesser extent, *The Book of Balaam's Ass*—exhausted Jones's need to write directly about his experience of the First War, the sense of 'getting into' history and of being forced to 'live' it, lies behind all of his later work. *The Anathemata* is, as I suggested in my opening chapter, articulate about history; but this articulacy is not the product only of self-conscious intellectual decision, or of large poetic and 'prophetic' ambition—as one feels it is, sometimes, in Pound—but of deeply felt *need*. History in *The Anathemata* is history proved upon its writer's pulses. 'In *The Anathemata*,' says Peter Levi, 'a sense of the identity of present events with ancient ones, which seems to have begun in the war, breaks wide open into an attempt to understand religion and tradition, but the position of an old soldier, his fraternity and his humanity and his direct understanding of a really terrible world, is never deserted.'[8] The 'position' from which history is viewed is one that feels radical sympathy for—and, indeed, identification with—those whom *In Parenthesis* calls 'the essential foot-mob, the platoon wallahs, the small men who permanently are with their sections, who have no qualifications, who look out surprisedly from a confusion of gear, who endure all things.'[9] And David Jones's historical sense, his position in relation to his material in the poem, locates itself—is, one might say, compacted—in his language. The several characteristics of the 'auditory imagination' which Eliot defines in the words I use as epigraph to this chapter seem to me accurately to suggest David Jones's central achievement in *The Anathemata*. And, with a view to indicating how such qualities of the imagination may be seen at work in Jones's poem, I want to spend some time here examining some aspects of its language.

I have already said of 'Angle-Land' that the subject of the poem there becomes its own mode of discourse and that we are confronted, in that section, with a 'drama of etymology'. To a lesser extent, this is true of *The Anathemata* as a whole, and the handling of language in 'Angle-Land' may be regarded as paradigmatic. David Jones's historical imagination discovers itself primarily in etymology: his extraordinary self-consciousness about language is the product of a linguistic interest that finds history vibrant and incarnate in the languages we speak, and have spoken. For David Jones, the realities of history, and the shape of the world, are perceived not *through* language but *in* it. Language in *The Anathemata* is recalcitrantly present, tangibly actual, insisting that there is nothing to see through *to*, there is only itself to be seen and heard. It is a tongue stubbornly conserving, hoarding and gradually unstoring its riches. In 'Rite and Fore-Time', the Willendorf stone is said to have been carved

> O long before they lateen'd her Ister
> or Romanitas manned her gender'd stream.
>
> (*Ana*, 59)

In these lines the flesh of the poem's language is bruised with the weight of cultural exchange made possible by the river Danube (the subsequent name for the river Ister). The feminine river is made masculine by the Latin language; grammar incarnates history. And all by means of puns which insist, in 'lateen'd' (as in 'using a lateen sail'), and 'manned' (as in 'manning a ship'), on the literal activities actually performed, throughout history, on that river. In 'Middle-Sea and Lear-Sea', as the Mediterranean sailors approach the hills of Cornwall, they watch the birds

> go leeward to the tor-lands
> where the tin veins maculate the fire-rocks.
>
> (*Ana*, 106)

The tin-veins maculate the fire-rocks indeed: 'maculate' is exactly the right technical geological word for what the mineral does to the rock; but the monosyllabic nakedness of the Celtic, Anglo-Saxon and Norse derivations is also visibly stained, 'maculated', by the imposing trisyllable of a plutocratic and conquering imperium. In such lines the coincidence of language and reality in David Jones is total: the world in *The Anathemata* seems to be discovered in the process of generating names for itself, of bringing itself to birth through language. Which is to say, I suppose, that for all his attempt in the early parts of the poem to imagine the processes of a world without humanity, David Jones's use of language constantly implies that the world has significance only because we can name it and speak it.

And it is precisely this obsessive interest in giving things their proper names that is the fundamental characteristic of Jones's language in the poem: *The Anathemata* is a quite exceptionally onomastic poem. Giving things their proper names involves the employment of a large vocabulary—from specific crafts and trades and arts, from other languages—that often sends the ordinary reader to a dictionary. But the effort David Jones demands from his readers will seem worthwhile if we return from the dictionary and reference books with an understanding of what the archaeologist Stuart Piggott has described as 'the process of inspired nuclear fission' which Jones applies to language; Jones's words, says Piggott, are 'radioactive with history.'[10] The difficulties of David Jones's vocabulary never seem pretentious or self-regarding, but the result of a loving, patient dedication to making the word coincide as closely as possible with the object it names. The instruction of the preface, that we should read the poem 'with deliberation', confirms what its typography also insists—that the essential structural unit of *The Anathemata* is not the line, or even the phrase, but the word itself. There is no other poem in the language that so clearly surrounds its individual words with space and silence. And this, of course, places an extraordinary stress of poetic responsibility on the words themselves. 'One of the efficient causes of which the effect called poetry is a dependent,' says Jones in the preface, 'involves the employment of a particular language or languages, and involves that employment at an especially heightened tension. The means or agent is a veritable torcular, squeezing every drain of evocation from the word-forms of that language or languages'. (*Ana,* 20) And, almost as an unconscious demonstration of what this might mean for such 'word-forms', Jones observes elsewhere of some early Welsh poetry that 'in some lines the words seem to thrust and thud and dilapidate to silence as though they themselves were the effect of what they signified.'[11]

This could perhaps be thought dangerously close to an almost magical belief in the capacity of a word to conjure a thing—dangerous for a poet, who must do more with a word than simply to *use* it—but the insistence of *The Anathemata* is, repeatedly, in the opposite direction, that a thing can be said fully to exist only in the names we find for it. When the poem's voice enquires, at the beginning of 'The Lady of the Pool', whether the sea-captain has heard the Lady's cockney (her '*East-Seaxna*-nasal'), it situates the city of London at the centre of its linguistic nexus:

> (Whose nestle-cock *polis* but theirs knows the sweet gag and in what *urbs* would he hear it if not in Belin's *oppidum*, the greatest *burh* in nordlands?)
>
> (*Ana*, 124)

London as Greek *polis*, as Latin *urbs*, as the Romanised Brythonic 'Belin's *oppidum*', as Anglo-Saxon *burh*, here, in this single parenthesis, is made to uncover the store of cultural and historical energy which it contains. The cockney accent is mined with the motion of the succeeding invasions of peoples and tongues which have moulded its 'sweet gag'. In 'Middle-Sea and Lear-Sea', the English channel is perceived, similarly, within the languages of those who have sailed it:

> Now nor'-east by north
>   now east by north, easting.
> Sou' sou'-west the weather quarter
>   by what slant of wind
> they brought her into the Narrow Sea
>   Prydain's *camlas*!
> that they'll call Mare Austrum
>   *Our* thalassa!
> The lead telling fifty in the chops.
>
> (*Ana*, 101)

The compass needle here, we might think, points to more than literal directions; it points also to the realities of the history of the English Channel, as this present Mediterranean craft sails through a Brythonic or Celtic '*camlas*' and transforms it into the Romans' 'Mare Austrum' or 'South Sea'. And the Channel is 'our thalassa' because the ideas embodied in thinking of the sea as thalassa—the thalassic imperial voyages of the Mediterranean—transformed this seaway, for the English, into the channel of their own imperial power. Such meanings are clarified further when the top-tree boy later cries 'from *his* thalassa over their *mare*' and the land they sight is not 'Britain' but 'Pretani-shore'.

The desire to name things in the language that most clearly 'incants' the complexities of their meaning sets David Jones's poetry bristling with unusual, exotic and archaic usages, and with his own neologisms, which attempt, indeed, to squeeze every ounce of evocation from their roots. These neologisms often take the form of a verbing of nouns into past participle forms—'gammadion'd castle', 'echelon'd Skaian', 'the fonted water/the fronded wood', 'the troia'd lanes of the city', 'her felspar'd war', 'the quartz'd height'. Such forms not only give Jones's language an extreme 'recession and thickness-through', an almost sculptured weight and density, a taut, muscular strength, but also suggest the impacted presence of a creative will in nature and history: if 'the bay's wide bowl' is 'darked' (*Ana*, 108), the implication is that someone, or something, has made it so.

The precision and particularity of Jones's language manifests, too, a desire to uncover a root vitality locked in the English tongue, in which, for David Jones, the language of Anglo-Saxon England is central. Jones can occasionally employ a pastiche of its kennings—

>   Drove of world-wind, sun's obedient daughter
>   hove down of wind, wave's mother
>   pooped of billow, son of wave.
>   (*Ana*, 107)—

but, more often in the poem, the Anglo-Saxon alliterative line provides a model for his 'free verse' or 'incantatory prose'. Sometimes the typography of the poem emphasises this derivation, as it splits passages into brief metrical phrases, heavily accented, in a system of deliberate checks and pauses, as in this passage of 'Middle-Sea and Lear-Sea' from which I have already quoted:

>   Extend your hands
>   all you *orantes*
>   for the iron-dark shore
>   is to our lee
>   over the lead-dark sea
>   and schisted Ocrinum looms in fairish visibility
>   and white-plumed riders shoreward go
>   and
>   THE BIRDS DECLARE IT
>   that wing white and low
>   that also leeward go
>   go leeward to the tor-lands
>   where the tin-veins maculate the fire-rocks.
>   The birds
>   have a home
>   in those rocks.
>   (*Ana*, 106-7)

The first four lines here employ the regular double stress of four Anglo-Saxon half-lines, and this rhythm is then freely adapted and developed through the passage. But I have decided to illustrate Jones's Anglo-Saxon variations with this passage, from among the very many in the poem that would make the same point, because it also conveniently demonstrates his reliance on typography, and his employment of a system of internal riming and chiming—based, very loosely, on Welsh *cynghanedd* (as were some of Hopkins's characteristic effects: the 'warm-laid grave of a womb-life grey' of *The Wreck of the Deutschland*, for instance) to supplant traditional English metric. Typographical arrangement here works towards emphasis and clarity; it instructs us in pause and stress; it shows how, exactly, to weigh words 'with deliberation'.

But this 'root vitality' of English which Jones wishes to recapture is not only a matter of returning to roots and origins, of returning there and 'bringing something back'. It is a matter, primarily, of working towards those fusions Eliot describes as part of the 'auditory imagination'—fusions of 'the old and obliterated and the trite, the current, and the new and surprising, the most ancient and the most civilised mentality'. The essence of David Jones's language is its adventurous and 'surprising' juxtaposition of different lexical registers. 'Probably no writer since the time of Shakespeare', Peter Levi has said, 'has brought to bear so wide a range of the English language and such different levels of it inside a few pages.'[12] The range and vitality, the evocative power, of David Jones's language is a result, perhaps, of his detachment and distance from the influence of twentieth-century standard, middle-class English usage. Educated, it would seem, only fitfully at a school, which he left very young for an art college, and never educated at a university, David Jones spent the formative periods of his life actually in, or in touch with, communities rooted in speech patterns more venerable and, possibly, more powerfully energetic, than those of a sophisticated literary culture. His tongue discovered itself in the 'otherness' of the Welsh language; in the cockney dockland speech of Rotherhithe at the turn of the century; in the living cockney and Anglo-Welsh usages of the communities of soldiers of the Royal Welch Fusiliers that he lived with from 1915 to 1918; in the Sussex village speech he would have known at Ditchling. And, further than these, Jones was, as we have seen, fascinated by marine speech and the terminology of navigation and seafaring, by 'tarpaulin language'.

The Golding character in *Rites of Passage* who uses this phrase also decides that 'Class is the British language';[13] and it is perhaps worth observing that David Jones's insistence on using forms in his work from well outside standard middle-class English usage has a specific social and political focus. The letters collected in *Dai Greatcoat* reveal that Jones was exceptionally self-conscious about his own place in the rigid gradations of the English class system. In one letter, written during the Second World War, he actually ascribes many of his neurotic problems to this anxiety and very revealingly refers to the 'excellent anonymity' of the army. His sense of his own anomalous social position ('neither flesh, fowl, or red herring') prompts a reflection on the nature of the war itself:

> It is absurd to say that Winston (for instance) *can* have the same reaction to the dropping bombs as the people in the Surrey Docks, and between those two extremes there are a million gradations—all mainly of an 'economic' nature at root. Death, mutilation, deprivation of every sort comes with a singular disparity on the 'rich' and 'poor'. The very nature of their fear is of a subtly different character. I see this very clearly. That is really what this war is about, a good bit.[14]

One wonders whether *The Anathemata*—which employs much more of the language of the 'Surrey Docks' than the language of 'Winston'—was not intended, at least in part, as reparation for the evasions and transferred social allegiances of David Jones's life. Certainly the language Jones uses in the poem, composite and synthetic, is a language heightened from natural speech patterns, embracing accents, tones of voice, intonations, musics, of enormous variety and dignity. The unforced naturalness of his cockney usages, especially in 'Redriff' and 'The Lady of the Pool', is particularly remarkable. They have none of that sentimentalising straining for effect that is so often inseparable from Dickens's use of the idiom, and none of the arms' length distaste, the *de haut en bas* detachment, that makes the pub scene in *The Waste Land* such a disfiguring indication of Eliot's lack of sympathetic inwardness with the language he mimics there.

The composite nature of Jones's language, in which cockney is only one strand, owes something to Hopkins and to Joyce; but its juxtapositions, its interweavings of the hieratic and the vulgar, of verse, catalogues, riddles, saws, folksong and ballad, sophisticated literature, technical vocabulary, liturgy and Bible, are imprinted with a very recognisable Jonesian stamp.[15] To recognise this properly is possible only within a reading of the whole of *The Anathemata*, for the *texture* of Jones's language is dependent on the elaborate building up of a full *context*, in which dialect and accent play a large part, the cockney speech of the Lady of the Pool and Eb Bradshaw mingling with the Welsh accents of the witches in 'Mabinog's Liturgy' and the more formal voice of other parts of the poem. For this reason, and simply because the poem is so full of voices (and, like Prospero's island, full of noises), it is extremely difficult to quote a passage that will convey a representative impression of this texture; but the following brief section of 'Keel, Ram, Stauros' may reveal the kind of lexical combination we can expect. In it we hear the voice of a member of the ship's crew complaining about the captain and about the ship's plutocratic owners:

> Listen: when it's adieu to y'r
> > Miletus ladies
> when it's farewell to you
> > Lady of Thebes
> when we founder
> > when we embrace the sea-stript dead
> wher'l they be?
> away with the coverage
> > on a proper siren's cruise.
> That's how they work it
> > in Pluto's Thalassocracies.
> Where'ld be their bleedin' miracle
> that is Graecia
> > but for us ones
> as cargoes-up
> > the thousand ships?
> Caulk it, m'anarchs
> > he's fixed you
> with his ichthyoid eye.
>
> <div align="right">(<i>Ana</i>, 172)</div>

This is a Greek seaman but, as Jones tells us in a note, 'My Greek seamen speak cockney'; and the whole passage does, indeed, demand a cockney accent. But this is, even as they go, a unique cockney Greek seaman who combines, in these lines, the rhythms of a sea-shanty ('Spanish Ladies'); the diction of sophisticated literature ('when we embrace the sea-stript dead'); the jargon of insurance companies ('coverage'); a mythological coinage for 'capitalist' marine enterprise ('Pluto's Thalassocracies'); a reductively cockney, cursing version of Poe's famous line in 'To Helen', 'The glory that was Greece'; a reference, in 'the thousand ships', to the Trojan legend itself; a memory of *Paradise Lost* in 'm'anarchs' (Satan is the 'Anarch old' in Book II); and, in 'ichthyoid', a usage that gestures towards the Christian significance of this sea-captain, the symbol for Christ during the Roman persecution being the fish (or *icthys*).

Nineteen short lines of text; and we find in them a wealth of reference and allusion, drawing on a wide variety of human experience and understanding, marshalled together and disciplined by the creation of a single speaking voice and a unified tone. This is what confronts us, with varying degrees of intensity, throughout *The Anathemata*: language, dense and compact with the history which has made it, releases the energy of its stored, inherited riches. And the voice releasing this energy here belongs to an anonymous 'cockney' Greek seaman. The 'history' available to him is a history of response to the will of others; the voice, silent in the history books, of one of those who 'endure all things' utters its complaint in *The Anathemata*. In this voice, and in the language which sounds and echoes throughout the poem, David Jones has, indeed, found what he calls in *The Tribune's Visitation*, 'hidden grammar to give back anathema its first benignity.'

This use of language, and the great wealth of material he handles, has led to David Jones's poetry being described as 'a struggle to talk about the history of the world',[16] and has been taken by many critics to announce an 'epic' intention in *The Anathemata*. For W. H. Auden, it is 'a poem . . . at once epic, contemporary and Christian' and 'an epic about the two Adams';[17] for John Holloway, the poem performs 'the authentic and traditional task of epic: to show a people itself from the very roots.'[18] Much of the discussion of the poem as 'epic' reduces, however, perhaps inevitably, to semantic quibbling: categorisation is made to depend largely on how much elasticity the critic is willing to allow the impossible word 'epic'. And it is consoling to find Jones himself insisting in a letter that he has 'not . . . ever understood what "epic" means, properly.'[19] Nicolas Jacobs is judiciously discriminating and helpful, then, when he describes what he calls a 'Virgilian' quality in the poem. 'It might be maintained', he observes, 'that, as far as the *Aeneid* is about Aeneas, it is little more than a pale imitation of Homer, and that it is only in the light of the *res Romana* as primary theme that the greatness of Virgil's epic becomes apparent. Virgil, that is, has brought to perfection a new type of epic. It seems to me that David Jones is using the *res Britannica* in the same way. It doesn't help in the least to be able to say that David Jones's poems are, or are not, epics, but if we can say that they have the same kind of epic quality that we find in the *Aeneid*, it may suggest ways in which we may profitably approach them.'[20] This is, indeed, the view of Virgilian epic that informs the writings of Jackson Knight, with which, as we saw in the opening chapter, David Jones was deeply familiar; and, in Knight's review of *The Anathemata*, he describes Jones's harmonising of complexities drawn from stores of racial history as 'a Vergilian method'.[21]

It seems clear, then, that *this* sort of epic quality does inhere in *The Anathemata*, and that the handing on of the *res Britannica*, the 'matter of Britain', which is peculiarly David Jones's through his personal inheritance of an Anglo-Saxon and a Celtic tradition, is what the poem actually *does*. Because much of this matter has become hidden, obscured, arcane and esoteric, *The Anathemata* is, of necessity, a very demanding poem; and it is an irony profoundly in keeping with Jones's view of the nature of artistic 'anamnesis' in modern civilisation that it is precisely the public, traditional 'matter' of the poem which has provoked the charge that it witnesses to a 'breakdown in communication'.

But there is, nevertheless, something a little disingenuous about Jones's insistence, in his preface, on the purely objective handing on of an inheritance which he defines as the poet's function. For a poet who believes that the artist should be 'dead to himself' while engaged on the work, David Jones includes a substantial amount of quirkily private and personal material in his poem. *The Anathemata* as a 'modern epic' is, despite its range of voices and styles, stamped with the immediately recognisable personality of its author. The poem, despite its frequently meticulous accuracy, its fidelity to observable fact, can sometimes be highly wilful and arbitrary. Although Jones 'officially' insists that the poet is 'a kind of Servus Servorum to deliver what has been delivered to him, who can neither add to nor take from the deposits', he is quite capable of supplying Aphrodite with a spear-fluke in 'Rite and Fore-Time' because he has some vague memory of seeing her so represented—and 'because, after all, a fish-spear is not inappropriate to her, whether as sea-goddess or goddess of love'. (*Ana*, 57) (The tendentious special pleading of that 'after all' may not correspond to the theory, but does advance the humanity of its author.) His incorporation of a Lancashire sheep-tally in the text is justified 'because it happens to be the only one I know'. (*Ana*, 76) He alters the 'Wallie' of his source to 'Walliae' in 'Rite and Fore-Time' for purposes of rhyme and assonance. One entire section of the poem—'Redriff'—is devoted to the monologue of his maternal grandfather. He neologises at will, and feels free also to vary conceptual language when it suits his poetic purpose, as when he modifies the Thomist *splendor formae*, 'to use it analogously and in a non-philosophical, everyday sense and in the plural' (*Ana*, 93), as *splendor formarum*. He takes the licence of anachronism: the voyages of 'Middle-Sea and Lear-Sea' form an impossible corporation for, 'although in actual historic sequence the Phocaeans displaced the Phoenicians as masters of the sea, in my text I put them in the same boat because they both were precursors of the Mediterranean thing in the lands of the Western seaboard'. (*Ana*, 105) He is willing to rely entirely on personal hunch: of his belief that one of the hills of Tegeingl signifies 'hill of despair or dereliction', he cheerfully notes that 'I can find no confirmation of this supposed meaning nor anything resembling it. As, however, that is the meaning I associated with it from an early age . . . I shall retain it' (*Ana*, 233). And Tegeingl is, in any case, introduced into the text at this point in 'Sherthursdaye and Venus Day' only because it was the birthplace of Jones's father—another 'objective' and 'traditional' association, no doubt. Twice in the text itself, Jones intrudes his own personal pronoun, once with an account of a reported Christmas truce in the trenches of the First World War, 'when I was a young man in France' (*Ana*, 216) and once in connection with the Second War at the end of 'Angle-Land'—'I speak of before the whale-roads or the keel-paths were from Orcades to the fiord-havens'. (*Ana,* 115) And many times he annotates a textual allusion with direct reference to his own personal experience: 'as recently as c.1935, when staying at Miss Helen Sutherland's, I saw, in Embleton Bay, boats with markings suggestive of the oculus painted in their bows' (*Ana,* 148); 'In 1949 I talked with an elderly Herefordshire farmer who vouched for the blooming of the thorn. He added that people he knew averred that the cattle knelt but that that was some long time ago and outside his experience'. (*Ana,* 206) And several cryptic references in the text demand lengthy explanation from immediate personal biography in the annotation, as when 'Bang! bang!! there were Julius stood-in for the South Foreland Light' (*Ana,* 149) is glossed as being based on the anachronism of an Italian recounted by a friend to Jones; and when he embeds in the text a very private version of Ennius by René Hague and elaborates in a note the circumstances that had produced this 'impromptu variation'. (*Ana,* 238) But—most unusual of all, perhaps, in a work that claims some sort of 'objective' authority—certain details in the text are, we are told, based on very private and chance scraps of information indeed: it is, to say the least, unusual to be told, in the course of reading a poem, that 'In 1912 in Camberwell a Miss Williams said to me, "On my father's side I am descended from Coel Hên Godebog." It is the boast of many old Welsh families'. (*Ana,* 70) *The Anathemata,* despite the efforts of some of its critics to make it seem so, is not, indeed, a solemn poem.

This body of private material, drawn not from any traditional 'deposits', but from the accidents of David Jones's own life and circumstances, drawn not from the 'objectivity' of racial myth and cultural tradition, but from the intense subjectivity of an outstandingly well-stocked mind, prevents us from reading the poem as, in any very available sense, an epic, even a Virgilian epic. The emphasis in *The Anathemata* falls not on the traditional material, the *res Britannica,* which it handles, but on the creative imagination of David Jones himself ordering, selecting, interpreting and transforming that material. The modern poet who would speak about history must, lacking a common culture in which to speak, speak also about himself: 'history' in the modern long poem is what the individual poet does with the necessarily fragmented data available to him. In those modern long poems which confront, and attempt to describe, a people's understanding of itself, what is being described essentially is the network of roots and attachments which define an identity for the poet. 'The history of one man's experience, if intensely recorded, contains the history of the race,' Vernon Watkins said in a discussion of David Jones;[22] and this desire to record intensely the junctures at which the self meets the public world, at which autobiography confronts history, relates *The Anathemata* to such poems as William Carlos Williams's *Paterson*, Charles Olson's *Maximus Poems*, Basil Bunting's *Briggflatts* and, perhaps, in a rather different way, Robert Lowell's *History*. Bunting and Olson work from a sense of the desire to preserve continuities in the face of an imposed discontinuity almost as anguished as Jones's own. The coda in *Briggflatts* articulates a question to which *The Anathemata* could be thought a response:

> Where we are who knows
> of kings who sup
> while day fails? Who,
> swinging his axe
> to fell kings, guesses
> where we go?[23]

And the opening of Olson's work makes a similar demand:

> But that which matters, that which insists, that which
>   will last,
> that! o my people, where shall you find it, how,
>   where, where shall you listen
> when all is become billboards, when, all, even
>   silence, is spray-gunned?[24]

And the terms in which Carlos Williams describes his undertaking in the epigraph to *Paterson* similarly strike an echo for the reader of *The Anathemata*; 'a confession; a basket; a column; a reply to Greek and Latin with the bare hands; a gathering up; a celebration . . . a taking up of slack; a dispersal and a metamorphosis.'[25]

All of these poems, with their very different strategies, insist that the primary theme for the serious modern poet—the poet most aware of what the first great wave of twentieth century modernism has managed—is, precisely, the search to find 'that which will last' and to reveal how that search proves sustaining and enriching in the poet's understanding of his own place in history. Olson expresses, in 'Maximus, at Tyre and at Boston', the way in which readers can best appreciate the nature of the effort being made in these poems when he writes

> that we are only
> as we find out we are.[26]

The Anathemata enacts for us the process in which one man, of enormously wide and often apparently 'eccentric' scholarship, and of exceptionally deep affection for the things of his own inheritance, explores what it means to live 'in history'. David Jones reveals, in his own searching, a paradigmatic pattern of the human intellect and imagination making sense of their place in the world. Reading *The Anathemata* is to be caught up in the fundamental processes of the renewing, creative mind as it reads its own understanding of reality. Which is the main reason that I open this study of the poem by claiming that *The Anathemata* is, crucially, a poem about its own possibility. The world contained in, and expressed by, *The Anathemata* is the world that this mind has made possible for itself. So that the poem is always attended by the consolatory gestures and adjustments and accommodations of the mind making itself at home in the world. Despite its anxiety and its sense of crisis, *The Anathemata* is, in the very best sense, a comfortable poem, a poem that has earned its own comforts and worked resolutely towards comforting in its turn.

The social and political relevance of the imagination's 'blessed rage for order' in *The Anathemata* is, then, that it attempts to define the self in relation to a complex of material—historical, literary, religious, mythological—that also defines the tribe. And it is, I would argue, Jones's achievement of localising, or domesticating, in a specifically British context, a modernist sense of the relation between a poet and his 'tribal' history, that has made his work influential on, and exemplary for, a younger generation of British poets. Forced by their own historical circumstances in the 'Great Britain' of the sixties and early seventies into a similar need to understand and cope with a difficult present, these poets also search through a past 'tradition' associated with a *mythos* of place, attempting to explore present suffering through considering the possible continuities and permanences of human value embodied in the history of specific locales. In John Montague's *The Rough Field* (1972), in Seamus Heaney's *North* (1975), in Geoffrey Hill's *Mercian Hymns* (1971), we can, I think, see a tradition being maintained, a continuity established, with David Jones's poetic effort and even, at certain points, sense the pressure on these sequences of a direct 'influence' from the preoccupations, techniques and strategies of *The Anathemata*.

The influence on Hill's *Mercian Hymns* can be sensed in its use of the form of prose-poems with annotation, and in certain of Hill's verbal manoeuvres: 'In dawn-light the troughed water floated a damson-bloom of dust' in Poem XXV seems to me, in its employment of compound nouns and past participle constructed from a noun ('troughed'), a very Jonesian usage. On Heaney's *North* the influence—or, better, to use Eliot's word, the affinity—can be sensed in his use of the Hercules/Antaeus myth as a pattern, partly, for the relationship between England as imperial aggressor and Ireland as native, plundered soil, 'dispossessed': such imperial/Celtic oppositions inform all of Jones's work. But perhaps the most basic strategies of *The Anathemata* also suggested to Heaney the possibilities of his myth-making, or myth-uncovering, in *North*: Jones's enterprise, Heaney has said, acted for him as 'a confirmation of proceeding by mythic indirection'; and he locates the central value of *The Anathemata* in its suggestion that 'the political role of the writer can be fulfilled in maintaining the efficacy of his *mythos*.'[27] And a Jonesian confirmation is also perhaps half-present to Heaney when his nexus of archaeology and myth is discovered at nurture in etymology, and he uncovers, or recovers, a world from a word:

> In the coffered
> riches of grammar
> and declensions
> I found *ban-hus*,
>
> its fire, benches,
> wattle and rafters,
> where the soul
> fluttered a while
>
> in the roofspace.
> There was a small crock
> for the brain,
> and a cauldron
>
> of generation
> swung at the centre:
> love-den, blood-holt,
> dream-bower.
>
> ('Bone Dreams, III')

And Jones's influence can be sensed in Montague's *The Rough Field* in that work's drawing together of poetry, marginal glosses from historical and journalistic documents, and woodcuts, in a literary *collage* which attempts to *read* Montague's own inheritance in a country where the 'whole landscape' seems

> a manuscript
> We had lost the skill to read,
> A part of our past disinherited;
> But fumbled, like a blind man,
> Along the fingertips of instinct.[28]

The nexus of myth, tradition, legend and language in which David Jones confronts his own 'Realien', and the heroic process of retrieval to which *The Anathemata* bears witness, has, then, offered an achieved thematic and formal exemplar to a younger generation of poets concerned, in our recent poetry, to speak about larger and more serious matters than the vicissitudes of the personal life—or at least to speak about the seriousness of the personal life in its context of the public world. If George Steiner thought, in 1967, as we saw in the last chapter, that *The Anathemata* was 'among prolegomena to future forms', it is possible to claim that these major poetic sequences of the seventies have realised some of the 'other potential orderings' suggestively present in Jones's work. This seems to me a profoundly significant achievement, and makes David Jones appear a much more inescapable and, indeed, more 'central' presence in modern poetry than some of the critical writing about him has so far managed to make apparent.[29] The character and scope of this achievement, if it has had to wait until recently for full recognition, has gained that recognition in the most unavoidable manner: *The Anathemata* has not inaugurated a critical industry, but has worked subterraneously on the sensibilities of other poets, and on their intimations of poetic possibility. The Lady of the Pool, after all, knows that 'what's under works up'.

But, however we situate *The Anathemata* in the course of modern poetry, there is one sense in which it unquestionably attempts an epic inclusiveness. *The Anathemata*, said Jackson Knight, 'does what Epic is meant to do. It gives a philosophic view, tenable for our times, of the secret places where nature finds reconciliation with the Divine.'[30] Of all the poem's attempted reconciliations, this is the one that finally matters for David Jones. 'In the course of writing *The Anathemata*,' he tells us, 'I had occasion to consider the Tree of the Cross as the axial beam round which all things move.'[31] Reconciliation with the divine is, in David Jones, a Christian reconciliation; and, if his is a Christianity that inherits, fulfils and embraces the other cults and faiths through which Western man has understood his place in the universe, it is nevertheless possible to say of *The Anathemata* what Jones himself says of *Piers Plowman*, that, 'though no work could be more belonging to this island, or be more rooted in a given locality and its people, yet, at the same time, no work could be more dependent on something other: the religion-culture, without which the poem could not, conceptually, have been. Not only the poet's "maistres and doctours" but everything within his purview is, in some sense, "under criste and crounyng in tokne".'[32]

But Langland's integrated, homogeneous 'religion-culture' is, of course, not Jones's; and, as D. S. Carne-Ross has observed, Jones 'is as conscious as Eliot that the Christian images have to be re-imagined if they are to get any hold on the modern mind.'[33] The Christian religion in David Jones is exactly the opposite of exclusive and sectarian: as Harman Grisewood has excellently put it, 'If Wales is for Mr. Jones the localisation of history, the

Christian religion is, so to speak, the localisation of human nature.'[34] In *The Anathemata*, familiar religious terms and concepts are always in sight—it could not well be otherwise in a poem that refers so insistently to the texts of a religion—but by something like what Leavis, discussing Eliot's *Quartets*, calls 'a subtle and resourceful discipline of continence',[35] David Jones washes these associations clean and renews them *poetically*. In a poem that contains so many proper names, the name of Christ almost screams its absence.[36] The making anonymous and generalised of references to the persons and episodes of the Christian story; the catachresis of mythical and Christian identities; the use of literal description to signal a theological meaning, without directly asserting it; the employment of a single vocabulary for describing art and religion: all are ways in which *The Anathemata* takes account of the heterogeneous culture in which it is written.

This process of re-imagining the Christian images impels *The Anathemata* towards a sacramental poetry: the otherness which its 'signs' point towards is an otherness present, and radiant, in the created world. Behind the shape-shifting and scene-changing of 'Rite and Fore-Time', the 'Master of Harlequinade' is discerned at work, and the 'New Light' beams 'from before all time . . . and with eternal clarities'. In 'Middle-Sea and Lear-Sea', the Mediterranean voyage is 'signed' as a traditional patristic image for the Church. 'Redriff' concludes with a celebration of 'the beams to which was lashed and roved the Fault in all of us'. 'The Lady of the Pool' reaches a climax in a lyric on the crucifixion and its redemptive meaning. 'Keel, Ram, Stauros' celebrates the wood that was the agent of that redemption. 'Mabinog's Liturgy' and 'Sherthursdaye and Venus Day' invite other mythologies into the world-dance around the Christian *stauros*. And the poem concludes in a celebration of the marriage between Christ and his Church. In Jones's imagery for the Christian mystery in *The Anathemata* there is a marvellous vividness and immediacy, and something of that 'child-delight' that he finds in Christopher Smart—'the "innocent eye" that saves, redeems, makes bright, the tough, sordid, impoverished grown-up world that we all know about and which is our common pasture.'[37] It is his refusal to be 'innocent' about history, but still to retain an innocent eye for the redeemed glory of the world that gives David Jones's poetry its peculiar and, I believe, its enduring quality. It is this uninnocent innocence in the poetry that allows Peter Levi to claim that 'David Jones shows us more than anyone in his generation, and more than Auden or Eliot, who we are and what we suffer.'[38] Jones's world is one in which 'anthropos is not always kind', but it is also one 'whose only threnody is Jugatine/and of the *thalamus*'; and the reeds and minstrelsy commanded at the end of the poem play the tune of a theodicy.

But, if the world of David Jones's primary allegiances—to Welsh culture, to the Roman Catholic tradition—can never be that of all, or even perhaps of many, of his readers, it is, nevertheless, a world that shows itself, in the poem, unified and coherent, a world in which the human imagination has lived and found enriching satisfactions; and the richness of David Jones's invention—what Seamus Heaney has called the 'opulence of his imagining'—is, for all its readers, as Eliot finely puts it in an essay on Jones, 'at least, a surcease of solitude'.[39]

Notes

1. Nesta Roberts, 'Sign of the Bear', *Guardian* (Manchester), 17 February 1964, p. 7.
2. *Gaul,* p. 128.
3. Quotations from *IP* in these paragraphs, pp. x, xi, 49, 174.
4. *EA,* p. 28.
5. *Dai Greatcoat,* op. cit., p. 249.
6. *EA,* p. 28.
7. ibid., p. 205.
8. 'The Poetry of David Jones', op. cit., p. 84.
9. *IP,* p. 126.
10. 'David Jones and the Past of Man', *Agenda*, 5 nos. 1-3, Spring-Summer 1967, 78.
11. *EA,* p. 57.
12. 'The Poetry of David Jones', pp. 81-2.
13. London, 1980, p. 125.
14. *Dai Greatcoat*, p. 107.
15. It is perhaps worth saying here that I think Jones's indebtedness to Joyce in *The Anathemata* has been exaggerated. It is really apparent only in some passages of 'The Lady of the Pool' which would certainly have been impossible without the 'Anna Livia Plurabelle' section of *Finnegans Wake*. It is perhaps an acid test of the strength of Jones's own poetic personality that he can adapt even such an idiosyncratically potent manner to his own purposes, without being merely overwhelmed. It is instructive to compare the early poetry of another major writer (though by no means a major *poet*), Samuel Beckett, who, in his poem on Descartes, *Whoroscope, is* so overwhelmed. See *Collected Poems in English and French* (London, 1977), pp. 1-6.
16. 'The Poetry of David Jones', p. 81.
17. 'A Contemporary Epic', op. cit., p. 71 and 'Adam as a Welshman', *New York Review of Books*, March 1963, p. 12.
18. *The Colours of Clarity*, op. cit., pp. 116-17.
19. A. T. Davies (ed.), *David Jones: Letters to a Friend* (Swansea, 1980), p. 89.
20. *Notes and Queries*, op. cit., p. 400.
21. See *Listener*, 1 January 1953, pp. 33, 35. The review is unsigned, but stated to be by Jackson Knight in G. Wilson Knight, 'T. S. Eliot: Some Literary Impressions' in Allen Tate (ed.), *T. S. Eliot: The Man and his Work* (London, 1967), p. 252.

Of particular interest to the student of *The Anathemata* are Knight's *Roman Vergil* (London, 1944) and *Vergil: Epic and Anthropology* (London, 1967) which brings together his *Vergil's Troy* (London, 1932) and *Cumaean Gates* (London, 1936). Jeremy Hooker, in *David Jones: An Exploratory Study*, op. cit., has discussed at some length the influence of these books on Jones's 'patterns of initiation'.

22. cited in *Letters to Vernon Watkins*, op. cit., epigraph.
23. Basil Bunting, *Collected Poems* (London 1968; 1970 edn.), p. 71.
24. Charles Olson, 'I, Maximus of Gloucester, to You', 3, *The Maximus Poems* (London, n.d.), n.p.
25. *Paterson* (New York, 1963), p. 2. It is worth noting that Williams was on the committee that gave Jones the Russell Loines Award in 1954. Writing of this to Ezra Pound, Williams recommends *The Anathemata* to him: 'It's a poem. Believe me, if you want something tough but rewarding, tackle that.' See John C. Thirlwall (ed.), *The Selected Letters of William Carlos Williams* (New York, 1957), pp. 324-5.
26. Olson, op. cit.
27. Private letter to me, loc. cit.
28. *The Rough Field* (Dublin, 1972), p. 30.
29. I am not, of course, claiming that I am the first to make this connection. Jones's work has been referred to frequently in discussions of these poets, and Nicolas Jacobs, in particular, establishes the relationship in 'David Jones and the Politics of Identity', *Agenda*, 11 no. 4-12 no. 1, Autumn-Winter 1973-4, 68-75.
30. *Listener* review, op. cit., p. 35.
31. *EA*, p. 39.
32. Letter to *Listener*, 4 April 1957, p. 564.
33. 'David Jones 1895-1974', op. cit., p. 704. Carne-Ross goes on to claim that 'one may think that of the two writers [David Jones] is sometimes the more successful.'
34. *David Jones: Writer and Artist* (London, 1965), n.p.
35. *Education and the University* (London, 1943), p. 88.
36. It does in fact occur once in the text, but there as an exclamatory gesture. See *Ana*, p. 92.
37. *EA*, p. 280.
38. 'History and Reality in David Jones', *Agenda*, 11 no. 4-12 no. 1, Autumn-Winter 1973-4, 59.
39. Eliot, 'A Note on "In Parenthesis" and "The Anathemata" ', op. cit., p. 23. Heaney's phrase is taken from the private letter to me already cited.

BIBLIOGRAPHY OF WORKS CITED

I By David Jones

(A) Collected

In Parenthesis, London 1937; 1963 edn. without illustrations, but with a Note of Introduction by T. S. Eliot.
The Anathemata, London 1952; 1972 edn.
Epoch and Artist, ed. Harman Grisewood, London 1959; 1973 edn.
The Sleeping Lord and Other Fragments, London 1974.
The Kensington Mass, London 1975.
Letters to Vernon Watkins, ed. Ruth Pryor, Cardiff 1976.
The Dying Gaul and Other Writings, ed. Harman Grisewood, London 1978.
Letters to William Hayward, ed. Colin Wilcockson, London 1979.
Dai Greatcoat: A self-portrait of David Jones in his letters, ed. René Hague, London 1980.
Letters to a Friend, ed. A. T. Davies, Swansea 1980.
Introducing David Jones, ed. John Matthias, London 1980.

(B) Uncollected

'Langland's "Piers Plowman" ', *Listener*, 4 April 1957, pp. 563-4.
'Message from Mr. David Jones', privately circulated address to the University of Wales in 1960.
Notes to the record, *Readings from 'The Anathemata', 'In Parenthesis', 'The Hunt'*, Argo PLP 1093, London 1967.
'Saunders Lewis introduces two letters from David Jones', *Agenda*, 11 no. 4—12 no. 1, Autumn-Winter 1973/4, pp. 17-29.
'Yr Iaith', *Planet*, 21, January 1974, p. 5.
'Extract from a letter to Fr. Desmond Chute', *Agenda*, 17 nos. 3-4—18 no. 1, 1979/80, pp. 273-7.

II On David Jones

Auden, W. H., 'A Contemporary Epic', *Encounter*, XII no. 2, Feb 1954, pp. 67-71.
Auden, W. H., 'Adam as a Welshman', *New York Review of Books*, March 1963, p. 12.
Berryman, John, 'Epics from Outer Space and Wales', *New York Times Book Review*, 21 July 1963, pp. 4-5.
Blamires, David, *David Jones: Artist and Writer* (Manchester, 1971).
Bonnerot, Louis, '*The Anathemata* de David Jones, Poème Epique et Eucharistique', *Etudes Anglaises*, Juillet-Sept 1971, pp. 236-56.
Bonnerot, Louis, 'David Jones and the Notion of Fragments', *Agenda*, 11 no. 4—12 no. 1, Autumn-Winter 1973/4, pp. 76-89.
Bonnerot, Louis, 'James Joyce et David Jones: Contacts et Confrontations', *Etudes Anglaises*, 53, 1974, pp. 223-42.
Carne-Ross, D. S., 'David Jones 1895-1974', *Arion*, NS, 1 no. 4, 1973/4, pp. 693-706.
Chute, Desmond, 'Anathemata', *Blackfriars*, XXIV no. 403, pp. 455-60.
Clark, Kenneth, 'Some Recent Paintings by David Jones', *Agenda*, 5 nos. 1-3, Spring-Summer 1967, pp. 97-100.
Corcoran, Neil, 'Textual Problems in *The Anathemata*', *David Jones Society Newsletter* no. 9, October 1977, p. 2.

Eliot, T. S., 'A Note on "In Parenthesis" and "The Anathemata" ', *Dock Leaves*, VI no. 4, Spring 1955, pp. 21-3.
Ellmann, Richard and O'Clair, Robert (eds.), *The Norton Anthology of Modern Poetry* (New York, 1973), pp. 559-70.
Giardelli, Arthur, 'Trystan Ac Essyllt By David Jones', *Agenda*, 11 no. 4—12 no. 1, 1973/4, pp. 50-3.
Grisewood, Harman, *David Jones: Writer and Artist* (London, 1965).
Hague, René, *David Jones* (Cardiff, 1975).
Hague, René, *A Commentary on The Anathemata of David Jones* (Wellingborough, 1977).
Heaney, Seamus, 'Now and in England', *Spectator*, 4 May 1974, p. 547.
Heaney, Seamus, Private letter to the author, dated 27 February 1977.
Holloway, John, *The Colours of Clarity* (London, 1964).
Hooker, Jeremy, *David Jones: An Exploratory Study* (London, 1975).
Jacobs, Nicolas, 'David Jones and the Politics of Identity', *Agenda*, 11 no. 4—12 no. 1, Autumn-Winter 1973/4, pp. 68-75.
Jacobs, Nicolas, Review of David Blamires, *David Jones: Artist and Writer*, *Notes and Queries*, NS, 20 no. 10, October 1973, pp. 399-400.
Jacobs, Nicolas, 'The Sacramental Scene', *Times Literary Supplement*, 4 March 1977, p. 250.
Kermode, Frank, 'On David Jones' in *Puzzles and Epiphanies: Essays and Reviews 1958-1961* (London, 1962).
Knight, W. F. Jackson, Review of *The Anathemata*, unsigned, *Listener*, 1 January 1953, pp. 33, 35.
Levi, Peter, 'The Poetry of David Jones', *Agenda*, 5 nos. 1-3, Spring-Summer 1967, pp. 80-9.
Levi, Peter, 'History and Reality in David Jones', *Agenda*, 11 no. 4—12 no. 1, 1973/4, pp. 56-9.
Littlewood, J.C.F., 'Joyce—Eliot—Tradition', *Scrutiny*, XIX no. 4, October 1953, pp. 336-40.
Mathias, Roland (ed.), *David Jones: Eight Essays on His Work as Writer and Artist* (Llandysul, 1976).
Noon, William, T., S. J., 'On *The Anathemata*' in *Poetry and Prayer* (New Brunswick, 1967).
Orr, Peter (ed.), 'David Jones' in *The Poet Speaks* (London, 1966).
Piggott, Stuart, 'David Jones and the Past of Man', *Agenda*, 5 nos. 1-3, Spring-Summer 1967, pp. 76-9.
Rees, Samuel, *The Achievement of David Jones, Anglo-Welsh Poet*, unpublished PhD thesis, University of Washington, 1969.
Roberts, Nesta, 'Sign of the Bear', *Guardian*, 17 February 1964, p. 7.
Rosenberg, Harold, 'Aesthetics of Crisis', *New Yorker*, 22 August 1964, pp. 114-22.
Shayer, David, Review of a David Jones number of *Agenda*, *Poetry Wales*, 10 no. 1, Summer 1974, pp. 80-2.
Spears, Monroe K., 'Shapes and Surfaces: David Jones with a Glance at Charles Tomlinson', *Contemporary Literature*, 12 no. 4, Autumn 1971, pp. 402-19.
Wilcockson, Colin, 'David Jones and "The Break" ', *Agenda*, 15 nos. 2-3, Summer-Autumn 1977, pp. 126-31.

III Others

Attwater, Donald, *A Cell of Good Living: The Life, Works and Opinions of Eric Gill* (London, 1969).

Auden, W. H., *A Certain World* (London, 1971).
Auden, W. H., *Selected Poems*, ed. Edward Mendelson (London, 1979).
Augustine, *City of God*, trans. Henry Bettenson with an introduction by David Knowles (Harmondsworth, 1972).
Beckett, Samuel, *Collected Poems in English and French* (London, 1977).
Bodkin, Maud, *Archetypal Patterns in Poetry: Psychological Studies of Imagination* (London, 1934).
Bottrall, Margaret (ed.), *William Blake: Songs of Innocence and Experience: A Casebook* (London, 1969).
Bunting, Basil, *Collected Poems* (London, 1968).
Clark, Kenneth, *Ruskin Today* (London, 1964).
Collingwood, R. G. and Myres, J. N. L., *Roman Britain and the English Settlements* (Oxford, 1936).
Coomaraswamy, Ananda, *The Transformation of Nature in Art* (London, 1934).
Craft, Robert, *Stravinsky: Chronicle of a Friendship 1948-1971* (London, 1972).
D., H., *Trilogy* (Cheadle, 1973).
Daniélou, Jean, *Primitive Christian Symbols* (London, 1964).
D'Arcy, Martin C., *The Mass and the Redemption* (London, 1926).
Davie, Donald, *Ezra Pound: Poet as Sculptor* (London, 1965).
Dawson, Christopher, *The Age of the Gods: A Study in the Origins of Culture in Prehistoric Europe and the Ancient East* (London, 1928).
Dawson, Christopher, *Religion and Culture* (London, 1948).
De la Taille, Maurice, S. J., *The Mystery of Faith and Human Opinion Contrasted and Defined* (London, 1930; 2nd edn., 1934).
Dick, Kay (ed.), *Writers at Work: The 'Paris Review' Interviews* (Harmondsworth, 1972).
Dix, Gregory, *The Shape of the Liturgy* (Westminster, 1945).
Eliot, T. S., 'Ulysses, Order and Myth' (1923), repr. Richard Ellmann and Charles Feidelson jnr., *The Modern Tradition* (New York, 1965).
Eliot, T. S., *The Use of Poetry and the Use of Criticism: Studies in the Relation of Criticism to Poetry in England* (London, 1933; 1964 edn.).
Eliot, T. S., *After Strange Gods: A Primer of Modern Heresy* (London, 1934).
Eliot, T. S., *Notes Towards the Definition of Culture* (London, 1948; 1962 edn.).
Eliot, T. S., *Selected Essays* (3rd edn., London, 1951).
Eliot, T. S., *On Poetry and Poets* (London, 1957).
Eliot, T. S., *Collected Poems 1909-1962* (London, 1963).
Eliot, T. S., *The Waste Land: A Facsimile and Transcript of the Original Drafts Including The Annotations of Ezra Pound,* ed. Valerie Eliot (London, 1971).
Frazer, J. G., *The Golden Bough* (abridged version 1922; 1957 edn.).
Frye, Northrop, *The Modern Century* (Toronto, 1967).
Fussell, Paul, *The Great War and Modern Memory* (New York and London, 1975).
Gill, Eric, *Autobiography* (London, 1940).
Gill, Eric, *Last Essays* (London, 1942).
Golding, William, *Rites of Passage* (London, 1980).
Hague, René, 'A Personal Memoir', *Blackfriars*, xxii no. 251, Feb. 1941, pp. 90-4.
Heaney, Seamus, *North* (London, 1975).
Hill, Geoffrey, *Mercian Hymns* (London, 1971).
Johnson, Samuel, *Lives of the Poets: A Selection* (London, 1975).
Joyce, James, *Finnegans Wake* (London, 1939; 3rd edn., 1964).
Kenner, Hugh, *The Pound Era* (London, 1972; 1975 edn.).

Kermode, Frank, *The Sense of an Ending: Studies in the Theory of Fiction* (New York, 1967).
Knight, G. Wilson, 'T. S. Eliot: Some Literary Impressions' in Allen Tate (ed.), *T. S. Eliot: The Man and His Work* (London, 1967).
Knight, W. F. Jackson, *Roman Vergil* (London, 1944).
Knight, W. F. Jackson, *Vergil: Epic and Anthropology* (London, 1967).
Kojecky, Roger, *T. S. Eliot's Social Criticism* (London, 1971).
Leavis, F. R., *For Continuity* (Cambridge, 1933).
Leavis, F. R., *Education and the University* (London, 1943).
Levertov, Denise, *The Poet in the World* (New York, 1973).
Lewis, C. S., *Arthurian Torso* (London, 1948).
Lowell, Robert, *History* (London, 1973).
Lowes, G. Livingstone, *The Road to Xanadu: A Study in the Ways of the Imagination* (London, 1927; repr. Boston, 1955).
Mabinogion, The, trans. Lady Charlotte Guest (London, 1877).
Mabinogion, The, trans. Gwyn Jones and Thomas Jones (London, 1949).
Malory, *Works*, ed. Eugene Vinaver (London, 1971).
Maritain, Jacques, *The Philosophy of Art* (Ditchling, 1923).
Monmouth, Geoffrey of, *The History of the Kings of Britain*, ed. and trans. Lewis Thorpe (Harmondsworth, 1966).
Montague, John, *The Rough Field* (Dublin, 1972).
Morris, William, *Hopes and Fears For Art* (London, 1882).
Morris, William, *Collected Works*, vol. xxii (London, 1914).
Olson, Charles, *The Maximus Poems* (London, n.d.).
Olson, Charles, *Maximus Poems IV, V, VI* (London, 1968).
Olson, Charles, *The Maximus Poems Volume Three* (New York, 1975).
Perse, St. John, *Anabasis*, trans. T. S. Eliot (London, 1930; rev. edn., 1949).
Pound, Ezra, *The Women of Trachis* (London, 1956; 1969 edn.).
Pound, Ezra, *Literary Essays*, ed. T. S. Eliot (London, 1960).
Pound, Ezra, *The Cantos* (London, 1964).
Pound, Ezra, *Drafts and Fragments of Cantos CX-CXVII* (London, 1970).
Rees, Alwyn and Brinley, *Celtic Heritage: Ancient Tradition in Ireland and Wales* (London, 1961).
Ruskin, John, *Works*, ed. Cook and Wedderburn, vol. XX (London, 1905).
Shewring, Walter, *Making and Thinking* (London, 1959).
Spengler, Oswald, *The Decline of the West* (London, 1932).
Steiner, George, *Language and Silence* (Harmondsworth, 1969).
Steiner, George, *Extraterritorial: Papers on Literature and the Language Revolution* (London, 1972).
Taylor, E. G. R., *The Haven-Finding Art: A History of Navigation from Odysseus to Captain Cook* (London, 1956).
Thwaite, Anthony, *Poetry Today 1960-1973* (London, 1973).
Tolstoy, Leo, *What Is Art and Essays on Art*, trans. Aylmer Maude (London, 1975).
Weil, Simone, *The Need for Roots* (London, 1952).
Williams, Gwyn, *Welsh Poems: Sixth Century to 1600* (London, 1973).
Williams, William Carlos, *Selected Letters*, ed. John C. Thirlwall (New York, 1957).
Williams, William Carlos, *Paterson* (New York, 1963).
Yeats, W. B., *Letters*, ed. Allan Wade (London, 1954).

Index

Andrewes, Lancelot, 68
Aquinas, Thomas, 8
Auden, W. H., vii, 28-9, 90, 104, 111; 'Compline', 72
Augustine, 43, 63; *City of God*, 50, 72

Battle of Maldon, The, 17
Baudelaire, Charles, 9
Berenson, Bernard, 78
Berryman, John, 1
Blake, William, 1, 17, 77
Blamires, David, 43
Bloy, Leon, 72
Bonnerot, Louis, 29, 44, 89
Book of Balaam's Ass, The, 29-32, 33, 96
Borrow, George, 78
Bradshaw, Eb, 56-8, 87, 102
Browning, Robert, 17
Bunting, Basil (*Briggflatts*), 107

Cara Wallia Derelicta, 14
Carne-Ross, D.S., 87, 110
Cavalcanti, Guido, 3
Cézanne, Paul, 9
Chamberlain, Neville, 33
Chaucer, Geoffrey, 17, 59, 63
Churchill, Winston, 33, 102
Chute, Desmond, 44
Clark, Kenneth, 3, 52
Cleverdon, Douglas, 87
Coleridge, Samuel Taylor, 17; *The Rime of the Ancient Mariner*, 75, 79
Conrad, Joseph (*Heart of Darkness*), 58
Craft, Robert, 39

D.,H. (*Trilogy*), 34
Dai Greatcoat, 32, 38, 61, 101; cited, 96
Davie, Donald, 3
Dawson, Christopher, 15, 46
de la Taille, Maurice, 9-10, 70
Dickens, Charles, 102
Dix, Gregory, 11, 85, 86
Doctor Zhivago, 37
Dream of the Rood, The, 17
Dying Gaul and Other Writings, The, 2; 'In illo tempore', 17, 57; 'The Dying Gaul', 17-18, 19; 'An Aspect of the Art of England', 75; 'The Welsh Dragon', 5; 'Art in Relation to War', 19, 94; 'Use and Sign', 21

Eliot, T. S., vii, viii, 3, 6, 12-13, 21, 28-9, 34, 38, 39, 55-6, 63, 72-3, 76, 83-4, 88, 90, 94, 97, 101, 102, 108, 110, 111, 112
Eliot, Valerie, 29
Ellmann, Richard, 33, 44
Ennius, 106
Epoch and Artist, main references, 2, 4-10, 68; 'Autobiographical Talk', 96; 'Art and Democracy', 66; 'Religion and the Muses', 20; 'Past and Present', 11; 'Art and Sacrament', 10-11, 78; 'The Viae', 2, 59; 'The Arthurian Legend', 16, 76, 79; 'The Myth of Arthur', 4, 79, 86, 88; 'James Joyce's Dublin', 20

Fatigue, The, 9, 49
Frazer, J. G. (*The Golden Bough*), 87-8
Frye, Northrop, 4

Giardelli, Arthur, 51
Gilchrist, Alexander, 1
Gill, Eric, 6-7, 8, 13, 20, 37, 57
Golding, William (*Rites of Passage*), 66, 101
Grisewood, Harman, 17-18, 110-11
Guest, Lady Charlotte, 15

Hague, René, vii, 16-17, 28, 44, 95, 106
Hall, Donald, 28
Harari, Ralf and Manya, 37
Hayward, Max, 37
Heaney, Seamus, 5, 30, 112; *North*, 108-9
Hill, Geoffrey (*Mercian Hymns*), 108
Hilliard, Nicholas, 75
Holloway, John, viii, 1, 42, 59, 68, 104
Homer, 21, 104; *The Odyssey*, 69
Hooker, Jeremy, 43, 83
Hopkins, Gerard Manley, vii, 8, 17, 75, 102; 'Pied Beauty', 75; 'The Wreck of the Deutschland', 101

In Parenthesis, 3, 16, 29-34, 39, 42, 49, 51, 57-8, 66, 70, 82, 90, 91, 95, 96
Introducing David Jones, vii

Jacobs, Nicolas, 32, 104
Johnson, Samuel, 42
Jones, Gwyn and Thomas, 15

Joyce, James, 3, 7, 8, 20, 28, 57, 75, 78-9, 87, 102; *A Portrait of the Artist as a Young Man*, 8; *Ulysses*, 39, 76; *Finnegans Wake*, 8, 39, 59, 65, 75

Kafka, Franz, 39
Kenner, Hugh, 12, 87
Kensington Mass, The, 49
Kermode, Frank, 3, 8, 13
Knight, W. F. Jackson, 104, 110
Kojecky, Roger, 12

Langland, William, 77; *Piers Plowman*, 17, 75, 110
Leavis, F. R., 5, 14, 111
Levertov, Denise, 90
Levi, Peter, 96, 101, 111
Lewis, Saunders, 85; letters from David Jones, 25-6, 27, 36-8
Littlewood, J. C. F., 76
Lowell, Robert (*History*), 19, 107
Lowes, J. Livingstone, 75

Mabinogion, The, 15, 67
Malory, Sir Thomas, 16, 17, 32, 70, 86
Maritain, Jacques, 8-9
Michelangelo, 21
Milton, John, 17, 19; *Paradise Lost*, 103
Monmouth, Geoffrey of, 15
Montague, John (*The Rough Field*), 108, 109
Moore, Marianne, 90
Morris, William, 3, 4, 6
Mussolini, Benito, 33

Nelson, Horatio, 56
Nennius, 25

O'Clair, Robert, 33, 44
O'Connor, John, 8
Olson, Charles (*The Maximus Poems*), 107

Perse, St. John, 28-9
Petrarch, 3
Pheidias, 51
Piggott, Stuart, 98
Plaid Cymru, 14
Plato, 11
Poe, Edgar Allan ('To Helen'), 103
Pound, Ezra, 3, 13, 19, 50, 76, 96; *The Cantos*, 27, 28, 29, 34, 87

Rosenberg, Harold, 5-6
Rouault, Charles, 9
Ruskin, John, 3, 4, 6

Satie, Erik, 9
Sandars, Nancy, 46
Savage, Richard, 42
Shakespeare, William, 17, 21, 101; *King Lear*, 62
Shayer, David, 39-40
Siculus, Diodorus, 75
Sleeping Lord and Other Fragments, The, 14, 18, 26; see also under individual poems
Smart, Christopher, 17, 75, 111
Spears, Monroe K., 28
Spengler, Oswald, 3-6, 11, 66
Steiner, George, 76-7, 110
Stow, John, 59
Stravinsky, Igor, 39
Sturt, George, 14
Sutherland, Helen, 106

Tennyson, Alfred, Lord, 72, 96
Thompson, James, 1
Thwaite, Anthony, 90
Tribune's Visitation, The, 1, 104
Trystan ac Essyllt, 51
Tutelar of the Place, The, 31, 67

Virgil, 68, 70, 86; *The Aeneid*, 65, 104

Watkins, Vernon, 16, 106
Weil, Simone (*L'Enracinement*), 15
Wilcockson, Colin, 6
Williams, Charles, 76
Williams, Gwyn, 43
Williams, William Carlos (*Paterson*), 27, 107

Yeats, W. B., 3, 13, 14, 64